I0815092

The God Layer

Faith Lessons in Real Estate

The God Layer

Faith Lessons in Real Estate

Ali Ban

For the Good Publishing LLC
Honolulu, Hawaii
2024

ForTheGoodPublishing.com

First hardback edition March 2024

Design by Donjiro Ban

Cover art by Erika Molyneux

ISBN 979-8-9896904-0-4 (hardcover)

Dedicated to my mother,

Thank you for inspiring every part of my life.

Table of Contents

Section 1: Seasons in your Career

Section 2: Seasons in your Schedule and Budget

Section 3: Seasons in Relationship with Clients

Section 4: Seasons in Transaction with Clients

Section 5: Seasons with Peers in the Industry

Foreword

Glenn Kelman

Eighteen years into running Redfin, I could count on one hand the books I've read about being a real estate agent. I have so much to learn from these books, but what puts me off is that many treat people as a means to an end, when each of us is an end in ourselves.

The authors of these books may be deeply spiritual people, but don't always bring that into a conversation about our calling. Since that calling is to shepherd others from one mooring in their lives to the next, through the birth of a child or the death of a parent, the beginning or end of a relationship or a career, it seems strange not to talk about the moral dimensions of our work. An agent can be one of the most powerful forces for good in another human being's life.

And this is why I love *The God Layer*, a book written by my brilliant friend and colleague Ali Ban. What makes the book a miracle is its combination of pragmatism and piety. As one of Hawaii's top-producing agents, Ali knows better than anyone the real-world challenges of being an agent, when a client gets cold feet or quits you for a competitor, but uses those moments as an opportunity to deepen our faith. No other industry has so many highs and lows, and *The God Layer* is a silver-linings playbook for how to handle every single one.

I hope you'll enjoy the book as much as I did, but in order to do that, you have to know what kind of person Ali is. She first came to my attention in the early days of Redfin, when nearly all our agents depended on our website to meet customers; Ali stood out because her customers all came from her personal network, and each one seemed to be a close friend.

Our business at the time had trials and tribulations, and the people in our tiny, far-flung Hawaii office must've become convinced we'd fail. It was Ali's unwavering belief in everyone around her that got us through those dark days. Whenever she walks into a room, everyone immediately feels better, before she has even said a word. If it were just a trick, I'd have learned to do it by now, but it comes from somewhere deeper than that. Ali is a very good person.

I wish I had known her earlier in my life. The closest I ever came to a great night of the soul was when I had to decide between attending medical school and running Redfin. I mailed an acceptance letter to the medical school, then got down on my knees in front of a postal clerk at a mail distribution center to get the letter back. I walked all over Seattle with my wife, trying to decide whether I should be "good" and practice medicine, or follow my passion, and lead a mission-driven real estate broker.

Blearily watching the sun rise behind the Space Needle, I finally told my wife that Redfin was what I really wanted to do with my life, even if I wasn't sure it was the most moral thing I could do. I was sure no one could deliver me from this miserable conundrum but then my wife said "if you do it, you'll make it the most moral thing you could do." Ali's book is a how-to guide for just that purpose! Had I been able to read it back then, with its steadfast belief in a higher calling, it would have saved my wife and me from a long, harrowing night. I believe the reason that you're reading *The God Layer* right now is that it might someday do the same for you. Keep it close by!

Sincerely,

Glenn Kelman

Redfin CEO

What is “The God Layer”?

Picture a layer of glass placed on top of a precious artwork for framing, or a sheer ornamental veil laid over a bride’s beautiful face. “The God Layer” is God’s purpose overlaid on our daily lives to make everything we do more meaningful. The God Layer elevates our earthly real estate work to His eternal work. Once we are aware of The God Layer anointing our work, we will see real estate transactions and relationships in a whole new light.

This book is for new agents, veteran brokers, and everyone in between. It’s for believers, skeptics, and everyone in between. Anyone who has worked with me will attest that I am not ‘holier than thou’. I walk alongside you, 12 years into my real estate journey and many decades up the hills and down the valleys as a Christian. I still have much to learn in both real estate and faith. I humbly invite you to join me to become aware of, and to activate The God Layer in our work.

The only prerequisite for this book is that **you care deeply** about your real estate work, clients, and industry relationships.

You can decide when to read each topical chapter, probably **not in order.**

Start at the **Table of Contents** or **Index** and let God illuminate the chapter He wants you to read that day.

Bible verses guide and teach us God’s perspective on each chapter’s topic.

I hope the **'reflect'** questions spur honest introspection.

Prayer prompts can jump start a conversation with God. Feel free to continue off script!

Each time you open this book and spend a little time with God, I know He will reveal His God Layer—His purpose and meaning—for your work. Pour your heart out to Him as He gives you daily triumphs and challenges. I pray that as you read, your heart will be the good, fertile soil where the living seeds of God's word will take root and flourish. May God bless your work and service in real estate!

Ecclesiastes 3:9-13 (NIV)

"What do workers gain from their toil? I have seen the burden God has laid on the human race. He has made everything beautiful in its time. He has also set eternity in the human heart; yet no one can fathom what God has done from beginning to end. I know that there is nothing better for people than to be happy and to do good while they live. That each of them may eat and drink, and find satisfaction in all their toil—this is the gift of God."

About the Bible translations in this book

There are hundreds of English Bible translations. Generally, they are categorized into three translation types or methods:

Word-for-word literal translations aim to stay true to the wording of the original Hebrew and Greek texts. These are known as **"Formal Equivalence"** translations.

In this book, the passages marked "**AMP**" (for the Amplified Bible) fall into this first category. One note in particular about the Amplified Bible: it can take some getting used to the extra words and punctuation. The Lockman Foundation, publisher of the Amplified Bible, gives this summary:

> *Without sacrificing accuracy, the Amplified Bible uses synonyms and definitions to explain and expand the meaning of words in the text by placing amplification in parentheses, brackets, and after keywords. As a result English readers can clearly and completely grasp the meaning as it was understood by the readers of the original languages with these most accurate translations. Additionally, amplifications may provide further theological, historical, and other details for a better understanding of the text.*

Thought-for-thought translations may stray slightly from the literal wording but remain true to the meaning of the original text using more current and readable syntax. These are known as "**Dynamic Equivalence**" translations.

The passages marked "**NIV**" (for the New International Version) and "**NLT**" (for the New Living Translation) fall into this category.

The third type are **paraphrases**, also known as "**Functional Equivalence**." They can be subject to the interpretations of the Bible scholar(s) who wrote them.

The passages marked "**MSG**" (for "The Message") are from a popular version written by Eugene H. Peterson. The passages marked "**TPT**" are from The Passion Translation.

Please feel free to use the Bible translation with which you feel most comfortable or familiar. But you might keep your heart and mind open and try switching things up periodically—a mentor and broker for a large Hawaii realty company, Cherie Tsukamoto, tries a new version every year! God's truths are transcendent regardless of the translation and have the same holy intent: to illuminate and grow our understanding of God!

Psalm 119:105 (NLT)

"Your word is a lamp to guide my feet
and a light for my path."

The most important thing

Better than money or success

Before I joined the real estate business, my Pre-Licensing teacher, Abe Lee, impressed an important lesson upon our class that had nothing to do with the contract or property: in the people-centric business of real estate, he taught us: "Guard your reputation."

Here in Hawaii, whenever we are surprised to realize we know someone in common we exclaim, "It's a small island!" Instead of six degrees of separation, in the real estate industry it can be more like one or two. We must assume that if we behave well—or badly—people we know will find out.

Whether good or bad, our reputation in this business precedes us. When we meet or talk with another agent or industry associate, they may treat us differently based on what they've heard about us. If we have a bad reputation (whether deserved or not), we must work harder from the get-go to earn trust. It's much easier to maintain and live up to a good reputation than overcome a bad one.

> **Proverbs 22:1 (AMP)**
>
> "A good name [earned by honorable behavior, godly wisdom, moral courage, and personal integrity] is more desirable than great riches; And favor is better than silver and gold."

My teacher's advice aligns with what the Bible teaches: a solid reputation is worth more than money or career success.

Reflect: ***Are my real estate career goals aligned with the world's values of silver and gold, or are they aligned with God's values of a good reputation and favor with Him and others?***

How do we go about developing a good reputation? The Amplified version of the verse above gives a perfect list: "honorable behavior, godly wisdom, moral courage, and personal integrity."

If we were to take a survey on the character trait most appreciated in a real estate agent, the top reply might be integrity. This is not an official definition, but I would sum up integrity in real estate as follows:

- Honesty in our communication with clients and industry associates
- Always having upright motives
- Consistently giving the same, best service we can to all.

Reflect: ***How can I apply more integrity to various daily real estate tasks?***

Do we promptly answer our phone or email? Do we follow up and do what we promise? Are we cooperative during a transaction? Do we communicate professionally, with kindness and love? Do we treat every client and industry associate with the same respect and commitment?

The beautiful thing is that if we strive to follow God's moral compass in general, we will simultaneously build integrity and good reputations in our real estate careers. If we do this, and are also known for our faith and love for Jesus, we can be powerful witnesses for the Lord! Many chapters in this book will help us recognize how The God Layer works through us so we can be beacons of His light in our industry.

Matthew 5:16 (NIV)

"In the same way, let your light shine before others, that they may see your good deeds and glorify your Father in heaven."

Prayer prompt: *Dear God, I want to dedicate my real estate career to you. As I work with clients and industry associates, help me to be honest in my communication, upright in my motives, and give everyone the same, best service. Give me integrity in my work in order to maintain a reputation that glorifies you. In Jesus' name, Amen.*

Starting at a new company

The emotions of change

Real estate agents tend to move around! I moved companies three times within my first four years. Whether you're a new agent joining your first brokerage or changing companies mid-career, a fresh chapter brings many changes and emotions.

One of the main emotions is excitement that this is going to be a great move! Perhaps we are looking forward to working with the coach or peer who recruited us. Maybe we chose this new company because of its reputation, training and support services, or better pay structure. We are optimistic all these things will improve us as agents and advance our career. We look forward to great results with hope.

Yes, inherent in a new beginning is hope.

Reflect: ***Where—or in whom—am I placing my excitement and hope?***

If we place our hope in a human being or company, sooner or later we'll be disappointed and frustrated. If we place our hope in our own abilities and strength, there will come a day when we are exhausted and spent. Can you remember a time you felt let down at a past job or company? The truth is, no other human or earthly entity can fulfill us for the long term.

Isaiah 40:29-31 (NIV)

"He gives strength to the weary
 and increases the power of the weak.
Even youths grow tired and weary,

> and young men stumble and fall;
> but those who hope in the Lord
> will renew their strength.
> They will soar on wings like eagles;
> they will run and not grow weary,
> they will walk and not be faint."

Reflect: *How does this passage make me feel?*

A new company, new coach, new co-workers, new policies and procedures—all this newness takes energy. These verses from Isaiah chapter 40 give us the secret to a source of abundant and endless strength: putting our hope in the Lord. The promises in these verses fill us with God's supernatural confidence. Isaiah 40 is one of the most rousing chapters of encouragement in the whole Bible. You may like to take a little time to read the entire chapter now.

Prayer prompt: *Dear God, as I read your word in Isaiah 40, I feel __________. I praise you because __________! Thank you for your promise to __________. Lord, increase my faith as I place all my hope not in any other human being or my own efforts, but only in you.*

Another common emotion we experience during a time of career change is <u>anxiety</u>. We may have spoken with several companies before making this choice. We worry; is this the right move? Not knowing the unknown is hard. But we can give our anxiety to the Lord too.

Reflect: *What am I worried about as I make this career move?*

Isaiah 41:10 (NIV)

"So do not fear, for I am with you; do not be dismayed, for I am your God. I will strengthen you and help you; I will uphold you with my righteous right hand."

As you start this new chapter, I pray you can turn both your hope and any anxiety over to God. In Him we have a constant and refillable source of comfort and energy!

Prayer prompt: *Lord, I cast my cares and anxiety about __________ in your hands. Whenever I start to worry, give me your perfect peace. As I move forward with this new company, help me remember that you are my limitless source of encouragement and strength.*

When you're on a team

Key ingredients for success or failure

Real estate has become a team sport, with some brokerages fully adopting this business model. There is a team leader—or 'rainmaker'—who is usually a more experienced agent and is responsible for finding and securing new clients. The leader may then partially or fully hand off the client or transaction to a team of support agents and coordinators. Team size can scale based on the volume of business, and each member's role may also vary based on the team.

When I first started in the business in 2012, I had the opportunity to join an experienced agent's team. I was 40 years old, and my previous job was as an executive at a local jewelry company. When I joined this experienced real estate agent's team, I brought my oversized ego along. Instead of being humble and recognizing I was in a totally new industry where I knew zilch, my pride prevented me from maximizing a golden opportunity.

The one crucial ingredient to being a successful team member and gaining knowledge and experience is humility. The one ingredient for surefire failure is pride.

> **Proverbs 11:2 (NIV)**
>
> "When pride comes, then comes disgrace, but with humility comes wisdom."

Reflect: ***Where have I faltered before in life because of my pride? In general, how easy or hard is it for me to be humble and open to others?***

When working with a team leader, we have a privileged insider's look at their workflow. In our business, there can be many different ways to communicate with clients, approach a negotiation, or organize our files. The more real estate agents we can observe and learn from, the more we can see the pros and cons of each person's style. All this experience will help us eventually develop our own style.

When we're on a team we represent our leader, so they may ask us to follow their way of doing things. Let's humbly embrace this learning experience. How they've run their business is what's put them in a position of leadership and success. Let's give them respect by taking lots of notes and following their instructions.

Reflect: ***What are the traits of this team and leader that I admire? Why am I excited to learn from this team?***

You may come to see your team leader's personality and style are different from yours—in fact, this may have been what drew you to them. As you follow their instruction and way, be open to leaving your comfort zone! This can be a great training ground for developing new skills and experience. You may not initially agree with the way they handle everything, but it's wise to keep an open mind...and possibly change yours. This is humility.

> **Proverbs 12:15 (NLT)**
>
> "Fools think their own way is right, but the wise listen to others."

Prayer prompt: ***Thank you God for connecting me with my leader, ___________. You have blessed me with this opportunity to learn from his/her guidance. Help me maximize every chance to learn.***

We may close our first few deals with help from our team leader. We may or may not get credit by name for the sale, and it might seem as if it's always our team leader's name in lights. This can be disappointing to our egos: we did a lot of the work; we spent more time with the client; so we should get the credit, right? I remember my disappointment at how small my first paycheck was—not only did I have to split the commission with my brokerage; I also had to split it with my team leader.

Because of my pride and short-sightedness, I ended up quitting the team in 2012. I muddled my way through on my own and learned the hard way. By God's grace I was blessed with help from other brokers and peers, but in hindsight, I would have set a stronger foundation for my career had I humbly committed to the team for longer than I did.

If God has guided you to join a team, it's a fantastic way to learn and grow as an agent. If you don't have a large sphere of clients, it's a way to work with real buyers and sellers under your team leader's guidance. Unlike working on your own in this lonely business, teammates bring camaraderie and can serve as a built-in sounding board when you need input.

Each of us has a career path the Lord has perfectly orchestrated. As you join this team, I pray it will be a fruitful time of learning and growing as an agent. May you be encouraged as God reveals His God Layer for you and your team!

1 Peter 5:6-7 (NIV)

"Humble yourselves, therefore, under God's mighty hand, that he may lift you up in due time. Cast all your anxiety on him because he cares for you."

Prayer prompt: *God, I need more of your humility. Please help me to see your God Layer purpose for joining this team. Transform any pride I may have into humility so I can be a great team player and witness for you. Thank you for providing this team experience for my career.*

Seeking mentors and peer groups

"No man is an island"

No matter how many years we have in the business, there is always someone farther along on the path who can teach us. It's always a good idea to have a mentor—or two or three! There may be someone at our company who is already a built-in mentor (our broker, team leader, or coach), or we can seek someone outside of our company. We should align ourselves with a few trustworthy mentors we can call upon when we need help or advice.

> **Proverbs 15:22 (NIV)**
>
> "Plans fail for lack of counsel,
> but with many advisers they succeed."

Reflect: ***What qualities do I want in a real estate mentor? Who are a few agents I admire and would like to learn from?***

We may gravitate toward a mentor who always makes time for us. A good mentor is also someone whose words and way of teaching resonate impactfully with us. Maybe we feel a kinship in personality, background, or values.

Seeking a like-minded Christian as one of our mentors can help us to follow not only the real estate playbook, but more importantly, God's playbook. When I started my career, God gave me a wise Christian mentor in Liz Garcia; she has decades on me in the business and knows the Bible intimately. Although we've never worked at the same company, Liz is someone I have turned to for advice at challenging junctures in my career. I will never forget that during my first year in real estate, she gifted me with an iPad I needed for my business but could not afford. I saw her Christ-like heart for her clients and peers and wanted to be more like her.

We can also intentionally seek out mentors who are different, or even opposite, from us. The verse above emphasizes multiple mentors because God created each person with a unique way and style. Advice from a mentor who thinks differently could be the key to opening our minds to a new solution we would never have come up with on our own.

Prayer prompt: ***Lord, I want to surround myself with wise advisers. Please direct me to the right mentor(s) you have chosen for me. Give me courage to approach and ask them to mentor me. If it is your will, please help them be open to working with me.***

Another idea is to form or join a small group of peers; you may sense more camaraderie when meeting with peers. When I first started in the business, I began meeting once a month with four other newer agents. Over lunch, we would take turns sharing what we had learned or were in the process of learning. We kept client and transaction details anonymous, but shared strategies, success stories, and learnings from our mistakes. These peers remain some of my closest friends even though it's been years since we stopped meeting regularly.

Proverbs 17:17 (NIV)

"A friend loves at all times, and a brother is born for a time of adversity."

Proverbs 27:17 (NLT)

"As iron sharpens iron, so a friend sharpens a friend."

Reflect: ***Do I tend to be a loner, or do I easily seek others out? How would seeking out a peer group improve my real estate business?***

You could 'kill two birds with one stone' and form a peer group that includes a mentor. You could also add a faith element to your group—starting with a prayer or short Bible study.

Real estate can be lonely work; during a transaction we usually work in silos. Having a mentor and a group of peers in the business keeps us from 'being an island.' This phrase originates from a sermon by the poet John Donne positing that we humans are interconnected and need each other to survive and thrive. Applied to real estate, regular interaction helps us stay on the right track on the job. The God Layer will also be activated as you deepen these mentoring and peer relationships.

Prayer prompt: ***Dear Lord, I want my real estate practice to benefit from other agents' wisdom and friendship. Please help me be intentional in seeking out a few mentors and peers so that I am not going it alone. In Jesus' name, Amen.***

When you need advice

How to ask for and receive counsel

Once we've established a relationship with a mentor or two, we should not be afraid to approach them when we need their advice. Fear or pride can prevent us from asking for help; our pride and situation will suffer even more if we make a misstep because we didn't seek counsel. Asking for a second opinion is always the right thing to do—for our own growth as agents and the benefit of our clients.

Reflect: ***How easy or hard is it for me to ask for advice? How easy or hard is it for me to trust and follow the advice I receive?***

> **1 Peter 5:5 (NIV)**
>
> "In the same way, you who are younger, submit yourselves to your elders. All of you, clothe yourselves with humility toward one another, because, 'God opposes the proud but shows favor to the humble.'"

When we are ready to ask for help, let's approach our mentor(s) with respect and humility. We should not assume they will always be available right when we need them. If you need an answer from them in a certain timeframe, make that clear up front. If your mentor tells you they can't meet that timing, it may be God steering you to ask another mentor.

No question is too small or unimportant: we can ask for help understanding the contract, getting through a snag in a transaction, how to deal with a particular client, or figuring out our career direction. We should give a full explanation of the situation; if we've made a mistake, our mentor will not judge us if we own up to it. Let's be patient as our mentor asks questions to fully understand the situation and formulate a response.

We may also seek a mentor's involvement when we find ourselves outside our area of competency. We can disclose to our client that we don't have experience in a certain area but know someone who can help. Our client will appreciate that we genuinely want them to have the best support. If our mentor joins us to meet a client, let's get out of the way and let our mentor lead. It will be an opportunity to watch and learn!

Prayer prompt: ***Lord, please help me know when and who I should ask for advice or to come alongside me with a client. Give me humility and an open heart and mind so that I can grow in knowledge and experience.***

As we receive our mentor's advice and assistance, let's continue to be respectful and humble. Let them share all their thoughts without interruption; take notes we can refer to later.

Some of our mentor's advice may be hard to swallow. It might be the right advice, but we are not ready or willing to follow it—yet. We can pray for courage and strength to know and do the right thing. God can sometimes speak or confirm His will through a mentor; but sometimes a mentor's advice might not be in tune with God's will for us. The Holy Spirit will give us discernment if we ask.

Our mentor may offer counsel that's unexpected or doesn't seem to address what we asked them about. Let's be open to receive any unsolicited advice—we all suffer from the condition of not knowing what we don't know. One strict lesson I remember from Pre-Licensing class is that all agents—whether new or experienced—are held 100% accountable to the law, even for unintentional mistakes we didn't know we were making.

Proverbs 11:14 (MSG)

"Without good direction, people lose their way; the more wise counsel you follow, the better your chances."

There are other Bible translations of Proverbs 11:14 where the emphasis is on listening to and receiving counsel. But I like how The Message's paraphrasing also uses the word "follow." What's the point of seeking advice if we are not going to follow it, at least to some degree? Chances are there will be some nugget of truth or advice that will help us. Remember, we chose our mentors because of their greater experience and knowledge. Let's be gracious for any connection we can get with our mentor; even this could be part of The God Layer.

Prayer prompt: ***Holy Spirit, thank you for helping me sort through the advice I've been given. If it's the right advice but difficult to take, help me find the courage to do the right thing. I want to reveal my blind spots and grow to be a better agent. Thank you for the chance to connect and learn with my mentor.***

When you're asked to be a mentor

Sharing our knowledge

My first brokerage had a few hundred full-time agents and several offices across Oahu. The company fostered a culture of 'paying it forward,' where experienced agents were encouraged to share their knowledge to help newer agents, who would in turn share knowledge with the next group of newer agents.

> **2 Corinthians 9:6-7 (NIV)**
>
> "Remember this: Whoever sows sparingly will also reap sparingly, and whoever sows generously will also reap generously. Each of you should give what you have decided in your heart to give, not reluctantly or under compulsion, for God loves a cheerful giver."

"God loves a cheerful giver" applies not only to money or material possessions but also knowledge. God has blessed us with our work experience and time in the business. Anytime we are given an opportunity to share knowledge with a peer is an opportunity to steward what He has given us and show love to our neighbor.

Reflect: ***When was the last time an associate asked me for help? Did I make time for them? Am I a cheerful giver of knowledge?***

We've all felt the uncertainty (or even panic) of not knowing how to handle something; we've also felt the relief when someone took the time to teach us. The busier we are, the harder it may be to cheerfully help when asked. Let's resolve to show a giving attitude by making the time to help—later if we're not free at that moment. Be encouraged by the fact that others find you approachable and respect your experience.

Prayer prompt: ***Lord, I want to be known as someone who is available and happy to help. If I am asked to help when I'm busy, help me find time in my schedule to help. Remind me that helping my associate may be part of your God Layer!***

We can help any number of associates with an occasional question or two, but having a particular agent formally ask us to be their mentor is a deeper commitment—a commitment that means meeting with our mentee(s) regularly and being available to them on call. We are choosing to forge an allegiance with this agent. It's a big responsibility and we should pray before making this commitment. We should also pray about whether God wants us to enter into this relationship with compensation.

Reflect: ***Do I feel called to be a mentor to ________? Am I cheerfully willing and able to make myself regularly available to them? Is it God's will for me to get paid (or receive a commission split) for my mentor role?***

A 50-year veteran in the business, Rod Mukai, is someone I've always admired for having mentored a group of seven top agents at my first company. Rod and his group studied real estate together, and they also performed acts of service together, such as organizing an annual "Thanksgiving in the Workplace" luncheon. As he began his fifth decade in the business, Rod told me he had thought to slowly wind down his business and not mentor other agents. But then he read Galatians 6:9 and it reignited his heart to continue mentoring. He recently started mentoring a new group of 7 agents!

Galatians 6:9 (NLT)

"So let's not get tired of doing what is good. At just the right time we will reap a harvest of blessing if we don't give up."

We may hesitate to accept a mentor role because we don't feel knowledgeable enough. But we don't need 50 years in real estate like Rod to qualify. In fact, it is healthy for mentors to show mentees that real estate learning is always ongoing. So, if there's a problem our mentee brings us that we can't answer, we can always bring someone else in to help us, then learn together. Accepting the challenge to mentor another agent will be a catalyst for our own personal growth.

One reason God will call us to become mentors is so we can show His love in these deeper relationships. Not everyone in Rod's former and current groups are Christians (yet!), but by gently starting each meeting with prayer, Rod invites God to be present in their meetings and relationships. There is no greater manifestation of The God Layer than this!

Mentoring is usually an unpaid job that takes time and energy. It is a selfless job as we invest in another agent's life and career. If we follow God's calling and do our best, there will eventually be a harvest of blessing!

Prayer prompt: *Lord, thank you for calling me to serve you by possibly becoming a mentor to ___________. If this is your will, help me make the time commitment in my schedule and the relationship commitment in my heart. Please use this relationship for your purpose and glory!*

Should you leave your company or team?

Hearing from God

It's common in our industry for agents to change companies. Maybe you turned to this chapter today because something or someone in your current company or team has frustrated you. When you joined, it seemed like such a great fit, but lately you feel let down and are wondering, 'Is the grass greener somewhere else?'

Or maybe things are going great where you are, but you've been approached by another company or team with an opportunity that seems promising. You're wondering if this other opportunity could level up your career. Is it time for a change?

Once we start thinking about making a move, there can be so many enticing options. How can we know where, or if, we should go?

Psalm 121 (NIV)

"I lift up my eyes to the mountains—
where does my help come from?
My help comes from the Lord,
the Maker of heaven and earth.

He will not let your foot slip—
he who watches over you will not slumber;

indeed, he who watches over Israel
will neither slumber nor sleep.

> The LORD watches over you—
>   the LORD is your shade at your right hand;
> the sun will not harm you by day,
>   nor the moon by night.
>
> The LORD will keep you from all harm—
>   he will watch over your life;
> the LORD will watch over your coming and going
>   both now and forevermore."

Prayer prompt ***God, thank you for always watching over my comings and goings. As I consider which direction I should go next, please give me clarity and guidance. Help me to be honest with myself as I go through these meditations today.***

Let's start by counting our blessings at our current situation. Surely God has worked many a good thing in your life and career in this current workplace. Can we still glean and grow by staying put?

Reflect: ***How has my current company/team been good to me? How do they continue to be a good fit for me? What advantages and benefits would I stand to lose if I leave them?***

There are many things about a workplace that take a lot of time and effort to cultivate—for example, a positive company and team culture, or mentors who have grown to know and care for you over the time you've spent there so far. Sometimes, once we take stock of all that's going right, we find validation we are still in the right place.

Next, let's consider anything that bothers us about our current workplace and see if any of these are true deal breakers when compared with all that's good.

Reflect: ***Is anything not going well at my current company/team? Have I ever been in a similar situation before in my life? What have I tried—and what could I try now—to improve the situation from my side? With whom can I have a heart-to-heart to try to troubleshoot?***

Proactively working toward repairing and healing issues takes commitment and maturity. It can seem easier to run away from issues. If we give up and jump ship, we might take our broken tendencies and bad habits with us. We may go to a new workplace and find similar troubling issues or personalities, with the net result being a new workplace but with the same old problems. You may take some time to pray about the situation or people at your current company; it's important not to rush this step of examining what could be repaired or healed.

Lastly, if we're still sensing the Lord calling us to a new workplace, let's consider what we might stand to gain by moving to another company, whether we've identified that next company or not.

Reflect: ***If I change companies, how will my clients and business be affected (for better or worse)? What benefits will I gain as an agent? How do I think God views my desire to change companies?***

Crossroads are a regular part of life. Psalm 121 above assures us that God never stops watching over our comings and goings. God has given us free will to make our own decisions. At the same time, He is standing by waiting, and is overjoyed when we ask for His guidance and direction.

Making time to be still to hear from God is a discipline, especially in our constantly plugged-in culture and technology. With practice, we can learn to identify the variety of ways God speaks to us:

- He may impart a thought, vision, or dream
- You may hear His still, small voice upon your heart during meditation and prayer
- He may point you to a fitting section of His Word
- He may speak through godly counsel from another believer.

Come before God and be still as you wait for His voice. Spend quiet time reading the Bible and meditating on verses He highlights. Ask a few trusted friends to pray for and with you. Changing companies or leaving a team is a major career decision. Whether it's to stay or go, know that God has an amazing future planned for you.

Jeremiah 29:11 (NIV)

"'For I know the plans I have for you,' declares the Lord, 'plans to prosper you and not to harm you, plans to give you hope and a future.'"

Prayer prompt: *Lord Jesus, help me to be still to wait on you. Help me be ready and know when you are speaking to me. Please show me the right path to take. If it's to stay at my current company, give me a new resolve and commitment. If it's to start a new chapter, guide me in the next steps you want me to take. In your name I pray, Amen.*

Leaving a company or team

Show loyalty

You've made the decision to part ways with your current company or team. It will please God if we leave on the best terms possible.

> **Romans 12:16-18 (NIV)**
>
> "Live in harmony with one another. Do not be proud, but be willing to associate with people of low position. Do not be conceited. Do not repay anyone evil for evil. Be careful to do what is right in the eyes of everyone. If it is possible, as far as it depends on you, live at peace with everyone."

If you haven't let your manager or team leader know yet, pray, pray, and pray some more before going into that discussion. Letting our manager be the first to know shows them the respect and honor they deserve.

Prayer prompt: ***Lord, please fill me with your love as I talk with __________. Help me to be mindful of your calling to shine your light, even as I leave this workplace. May the work of your God Layer continue there! Although I am worried about __________, I know you are with me and will give me the right words and heart.***

As you talk with your manager and colleagues, maximize this golden opportunity to recognize and thank each person. Remind them how they've blessed you and the impact they've had. Let's leave with a glow of genuine gratitude.

Reflect: *Who has contributed to my learning and success at this company or team? What are the specific things I can thank each person for before I leave?*

This is also a chance to humbly examine if there's any unfinished business God wants you to resolve. From whom do you need to ask forgiveness? Whom have you not forgiven but should? Now is the best time to make that phone call or schedule that coffee meeting. If you don't take the chance now, it may never happen, and the wounds will fester. Satan will surely take advantage of any leftover divisions.

It might be too early to start the healing process with a certain co-worker. The wound might be too fresh, or one or both of you may not be quite ready. Pray and seek if there is a small first step you can take now to leave the door open for future reconciliation.

Prayer prompt: *Lord, do I have any unfinished business before I go? Who do I need to talk or meet with? Please help me initiate reconciliation as much as possible before I go.*

Proverbs 3:3-4 (NIV)

"Let love and faithfulness never leave you;
bind them around your neck,
write them on the tablet of your heart.
Then you will win favor and a good name
in the sight of God and man."

Ironically, the thing you will need most as you leave is loyalty. I like this Dictionary.com definition of 'loyal': "giving or showing firm and constant support or allegiance to a person or institution." The key word is "constant," and here I believe it means we should continue our support long after we've left.

Reflect: *How can I put loyalty into action as I say goodbye?*

We will be asked now and later why you are leaving or left. Let's protect our colleagues' best interests: keep confidential and silent any thoughts about this company or team that might be perceived as negative or critical. Instead, let's go out of our way to find positive things to tell others; this will show our continued respect and loyalty.

Another way to continue to support our former colleagues is to stay in communication and on good terms. In this business, our paths will continue to cross. It's very likely someday we will present an offer on one of their listings, or vice versa. If we leave with grace and on good terms, our personal history with past co-workers will not encroach upon our client's chances.

I pray that God gives you a gracious heart as you leave your workplace. Some may not take the news well. Do your best to convey love and gratitude to them, and let God handle the rest.

Prayer prompt: *Thank you for guiding me during this transition. Please help me do the work to close this chapter as well as possible. Bless me with your favor so I can finish this chapter of my career well.*

When you're forced to leave a company

God is ten steps ahead

Receiving notice from your company that they are terminating your employment or laying you off is always a shock, even if you've received previous hints or warnings. We like to be in control of our lives, and don't appreciate it when someone else forces us in a direction we weren't planning.

There are so many emotions you might be feeling. You may feel abandoned or lost because you have no idea where to go next. You may feel anger and want to point fingers at the company. You may feel self-doubt and begin questioning whether real estate is the right career. You may feel relief, even if you can't quite pinpoint why. It's probably very hard to see The God Layer.

Reflect: ***Make a list of all the emotions you are feeling—good, bad, and ugly.***

Prayer is a vehicle for telling God everything with brutal honesty. We can cry out to Him, even if it's in anger or defiance. Whatever mix of feelings is on your list, you can express them in direct conversation with the Lord.

Prayer prompt: ***Well, God, as you already know, this happened: __________. I am feeling __________ and __________. I also feel __________ and __________ because __________. More than anyone, you know all that has happened, and you understand me. Thank you for letting me cry out to you as I figure out what to do next. Comfort me with promises in your Word today.***

The Bible can comfort us, and eventually change our feelings of shock and helplessness into resolve and hope. God has not abandoned us! He will be the source of our strength in the days and decisions ahead.

Psalm 118:4-8 (AMP)

"Oh let those who [reverently] fear the LORD, say, 'His loving kindness endures forever.'
Out of my distress I called on the LORD; The LORD answered me and set me free.
The LORD is on my side; I will not fear. What can [mere] man do to me?
The LORD is on my side, He is among those who help me;
Therefore I will look [in triumph] on those who hate me.
It is better to take refuge in the LORD than to trust in man."

Reflect: *How does Psalm 118 make me feel?*

We know God loves us and is for us; He would never throw us a curveball to harm us. Could this change be a blessing in disguise? What is the better path God is planning for you next? Be very confident; He does have a plan for you! In the meantime, take refuge in Him.

If God has something entirely different from real estate sales in His plan for you, that direction may also become clearer as you pray and seek Him. I've always marveled at how a real estate license can apply to so many different jobs—God may still have plans to use your license and sales experience in a different area of our industry.

Psalm 112:7 (NLT)

"They do not fear bad news; they confidently trust the LORD to care for them."

Prayer prompt: *Dear Jesus, give me a steady and trusting heart. I know you have a better plan for me, Lord. What is my next step? Who should I talk to?*

God will bring someone to mind—maybe a peer or mentor. God may even prompt someone to call you today! Remember that God has known this was going to happen and has already been at work on your behalf. Explore and pray through all the options God gives you. He may make it very clear by giving you just one option.

I trust that God has already begun to calm your emotions. This will be an exciting time as God increases your faith. God is ten steps ahead of you; don't worry! He is going to meet your needs within the time frame for your next move to be made.

Reflect: ***Take your original list of emotions. Cross off the ones that have gone away or diminished. Continue to pray through any that remain.***

I encourage you not to wallow in any harmful emotions that may remain on your list. Wallowing would give Satan too easy a target. To paraphrase Paul in Romans 8:37, you are more than a conqueror because of God's love! You will not be consumed!

Lamentations 3:22-25 (AMP)

"It is because of the Lord's lovingkindnesses that we are not consumed,
Because His [tender] compassions never fail.
They are new every morning;
Great and beyond measure is Your faithfulness.
'The Lord is my portion and my inheritance,' says my soul;
'Therefore I have hope in Him and wait expectantly for Him.'
The Lord is good to those who wait [confidently] for Him,
To those who seek Him [on the authority of God's word]."

Prayer prompt: *Lord, I claim the promise in Psalm 118 that you are always on my side. I claim the promise in Psalm 112 that you will take care of me. And I claim the promise in Lamentations 3 that you are good to those who seek you. Please increase my faith, Lord. In Jesus' name, Amen.*

Winning in real estate

Who's handing out the prizes?

Our industry usually measures an agent's success by how many sales we close. Our company tracks monthly and yearly statistics, deems which agents are winning, and hands out the top producer awards at sales meetings.

To this end, our sales coach may advise us how to prioritize our list of clients so we can make more sales sooner rather than later. Whenever we meet a prospective client, we are taught to add them to our pipeline and evaluate how soon they might list their home or be ready to make an offer. Many encounters we have may not result in an immediate sale for us; some may never result in a sale. My first sales coach advised me to be efficient and spend the most time with clients who are ready, willing, and able to close a deal.

Reflect: ***How do I prioritize the clients I focus my time and efforts on? How do I measure success in my career?***

What if God puts clients on our path or schedule not for a sale but for *His* reasons and purposes - His God Layer? What if the time we spend with them is what counts in God's eyes? God measures our success not based on our sales statistics, but on how well we follow His commands. We may 'fail' to achieve our earthly boss's expectations, but still 'win' as we strive to achieve our heavenly Boss's master plan.

John 13:34-35 (NIV)

"'A new command I give you: Love one another. As I have loved you, so you must love one another. By this everyone will know that you are my disciples, if you love one another.'"

Matthew 28:18-20 (NIV)

"Then Jesus came to them and said, 'All authority in heaven and on earth has been given to me. Therefore go and make disciples of all nations, baptizing them in the name of the Father and of the Son and of the Holy Spirit, and teaching them to obey everything I have commanded you. And surely I am with you always, to the very end of the age.'"

The God Layer is when God allows us to do His eternal work simultaneously with our daily real estate tasks. In order to follow Jesus' commands to spread God's love and message of salvation, we should look out for the people God has prepared for us. We must always be ready to be a witness for the Lord. There will come a day when God gives us the opportunity to pray with someone to accept Jesus—that is the ultimate win!

Prayer prompt: ***Lord, I don't want to dismiss or overlook any client because I don't feel they are a serious buyer or seller. Help me show love to each person you send me. Let me be mindful of your 'pipeline' of people to whom you want me to witness. Who do you want me to reach out to today, Lord?***

God often shows favor to His people in the form of worldly recognition and success. If God chooses to bless us with lots of sales or an award at the company meeting, let's ensure that as we 'win' in the world's way, we continue to win in God's way. God doesn't give us these human accolades for our benefit—God wants us to use them to shine His light.

> **2 Corinthians 4:7 (NLT)**
>
> "We now have this light shining in our hearts, but we ourselves are like fragile clay jars containing this great treasure. This makes it clear that our great power is from God, not from ourselves."

I love Paul's analogy here that each of us is a frail jar of clay, but we hold the mighty treasure and power of the Lord inside of us. We are just the container; God is the actual source of talent and anything award-winning within us.

When God wants to use an award for His glory, let's be good stewards of the assignment. The award and spotlight may become a catalyst for a conversation where we can share our testimony. May He give us the right words and attitude when that time comes. Let's focus our boasting solely on God's love and goodness to us.

> **Galatians 6:14 (TPT)**
>
> "May my only boast be found in the cross of our Lord Jesus Christ."

Prayer prompt: *Dear God, I acknowledge that you are the one who ultimately decides if I have done a good job in my career and life. I give you all the credit for any success in my life! Thank you for __________. Thank you for using me as your vessel to share your good news with others.*

Should you leave the business or retire?

Is God finished here?

They say that if you choose a job you love, you'll never have to work a day in your life. On many days in real estate, we find so much fulfillment that it truly doesn't feel like work! Serving people is always fulfilling. But there can be exhausting days when the pressures of the job close in on us. There are some days it's hard to feel passionate about this job.

This chapter is for you if:

- ~ It's been a particularly rough day or week on the job and you're pondering leaving real estate
- ~ Business is slow and you're not sure this job is sustainable
- ~ You're perfectly content with the job but feel God might be calling you to retirement or another ministry.

Prayer prompt: ***Dear Lord, I have a lot on my mind today: __________, and __________. Thank you for always being near to listen. If you still have a mission for me in real estate, please spark my servant heart and send me the people you want me to serve. Or, if you are ready to end the real estate chapters of my life, please reassure me that this is your will.***

Matthew 25:23 (NLT)

"The master said, 'Well done, my good and faithful servant. You have been faithful in handling this small amount, so now I will give you many more responsibilities. Let's celebrate together!'"

Reflect: ***If I were to leave real estate now, would God say the words above to me? Have I been his good and faithful servant in my work?***

As long as God continues to bless us with clients and transactions, chances are He wants us to remain in the business. However, just because you don't have any active clients right now doesn't mean God wants you to give up. He orchestrates these lulls between clients perfectly—perhaps the Lord wants you to rest and trust in Him to provide.

The passage below shows how God will continue to grow and prosper us even in 'old age.'

Psalm 92:12-15 (AMP)

"The righteous will flourish like the date palm [long-lived, upright and useful];
They will grow like a cedar in Lebanon [majestic and stable].
Planted in the house of the Lord,
They will flourish in the courts of our God.
[Growing in grace] they will still thrive and bear
fruit and prosper in old age;

> They will flourish and be vital and fresh [rich in trust and love and contentment];
> [They are living memorials] to declare that the Lord is upright and faithful [to His promises]; He is my rock, and there is no unrighteousness in Him."

Reflect: ***Is my business flourishing like the trees in this psalm? Do I feel God's continued blessing on my business?***

In 2014—my third year in the business—I met a Honolulu agent named Stewart Wade. He was being honored at a Honolulu Board of Realtors luncheon as he turned 100. Mr. Wade was still working part-time every day; his routine was to swim in the ocean in the morning before going to the office for a few hours.

I had the honor of chatting with Mr. Wade and he advised me, "Never do this work for the money; do it for the relationships." This matched my mission statement exactly but hearing it from this veteran agent validated and honed my purpose.

Indeed, one of God's purposes for us is to have fruitful relationships with our clients and colleagues. Of course, these relationships can continue outside of real estate, but this may take more intention and effort if we leave the business.

Mr. Wade passed away in 2019 at the age of 104, after 50 years in the business. I'm sure he had his fair share of tough days, demanding clients, and dry spells with no escrows. But he clearly believed that the fulfillment which comes from our relationships is worth pushing through those tough times. I don't think he ever officially retired. It's rare, but is this the model of retirement God has for you? Never actually retiring?

Rick Warren, founding pastor of Saddleback Church and author of *A Purpose Driven Life*, recorded a broadcast titled "Courage to Follow Your Calling," in which he points out that the word 'retirement' never appears in the Bible. Then Pastor Rick paraphrased his life verse:

> **Acts 13:36 (Rick Warren paraphrase)**
>
> "After (David) had served the purpose of God in his generation, he died."

Of all the inspirational verses in the Bible to choose from, isn't it odd that this would be Rick Warren's life verse? But this verse is deep in its succinct simplicity: We serve God during our appointed time, and then we die. Essentially, we should never stop serving God every day of our life.

That said, God may be preparing to launch you into a new mission field. This chapter's title question is: "Is God finished here?" "Here" is the key word—because God will never be finished working through you until He calls you home! His calling just might not be in real estate anymore.

Reflect: *Is there another mission field where God might want me to serve Him?*

Prayer prompt: *Lord, I want to continue to fulfill your purpose for me in life. Please help me to know if real estate is still your mission field for me, or if you are calling me elsewhere. God, I want to continue to serve you until the day you call me home!*

Retiring from real estate

God's sovereign, perfect plan

Moses had one of the most glorious 'careers' in the Bible—spanning 40 years (between the ages of 80 and 120) when he led the revolt against Pharoah, delivered the Israelites from Egypt, and guided them through the desert. Along the way, he was one of only a handful of humans to ever come face-to-face with God when he was given the task of hand-delivering God's law.

The Promised Land had been the end goal of Moses' entire career, so it was only natural for him to feel he had earned the right to enter it. God became angry with Moses for his repeated requests to do so. God ordained and oversaw the beginning, middle, and end of Moses' career. Just as Moses was bringing God's people to the border of their promised land, God forced him to retire.

Deuteronomy 3:23-28 (NIV)

"At that time I pleaded with the LORD: 'Sovereign LORD, you have begun to show to your servant your greatness and your strong hand. For what god is there in heaven or on earth who can do the deeds and mighty works you do? Let me go over and see the good land beyond the Jordan—that fine hill country and Lebanon.' But because of you the LORD was angry with me and would not listen to me. 'That is enough,' the LORD said. 'Do not speak to me anymore about this mat-

> ter. Go up to the top of Pisgah and look west and north and south and east. Look at the land with your own eyes, since you are not going to cross this Jordan. But commission Joshua, and encourage and strengthen him, for he will lead this people across and will cause them to inherit the land that you will see.'"

Reflect: ***How do I feel about how God ended Moses' career? Does the way Moses' career ended change the substance of his entire career? How is my career's final chapter similar to or different from Moses'?***

Like Moses, we may be having difficulty letting go of our career and acknowledging it's time to retire. Just as there never seems to be a good time to take a vacation in our business, there may never seem to be a convenient time to retire.

If we read on in Deuteronomy, we see that the ending of Moses' career paved the way for Joshua's turn to be used by God. God ordains us for our work in our time. Our unfinished loose ends in the business will become the seeds for God to work through another agent's life.

Reflect: ***Am I afraid—or excited—to let go and pass the baton? What is my succession plan—who does God want to help my clients going forward?***

Just as God prepared Joshua to follow Moses, a crucial part of our exit plan should be to choose a trusted agent to continue in our place. To give this agent who is taking the baton from us the best chance at success, we can do a warm hand-off and cheer them on—from the sidelines. We chose them because we know they will value and help our clients in the same caring way we have; so let's trust them and gently let go of our clients.

Ecclesiastes 3:11 (NIV)

"He has made everything beautiful in its time. He has also set eternity in the human heart; yet no one can fathom what God has done from beginning to end."

Like Moses, when God's perfectly planned timing for our retirement comes, we must accept His sovereignty. Like Moses, God's plan for our retirement may not be exactly what we hoped for or envisioned; however, we must have faith that this is exactly how God wants it. Like Moses, whatever our final chapter looks like, it doesn't define or detract from all we have accomplished.

Blessings on you as you explore God's next mission for your life!

Revelation 14:13 (MSG)

"I heard a voice out of Heaven, 'Write this: Blessed are those who die in the Master from now on; how blessed to die that way!' 'Yes,' says the Spirit, 'and blessed rest from their hard, hard work. None of what they've done is wasted; God blesses them for it all in the end.'"

Prayer prompt: *Lord, thank you for giving me a blessed career in real estate. Thank you for ___________. As I say goodbye, I feel ___________. I claim your promise in Revelation 14:13 that the good deeds I've done for you in my real estate career will stay with me always. In your name, Amen.*

Setting goals

Choosing a life or career verse

Every November at my first brokerage, the coaches directed us agents to create sales goals and vision boards for the coming year. The sales goals mapped out how many clients and escrows we needed to achieve our desired income; we worked backwards from our yearly goal to set daily, weekly, and monthly tasks. The vision boards motivated us with photos of the things and experiences we wanted to attain with our desired income.

In my fourth year in the business, my goal was something like, "Every month, I will meet 10 new clients, write five offers or listing agreements, and open two to three new escrows in order to close 30 transactions for the year." It was ambitious! I think I ended up closing 17 sales that year. But the coaches wanted to see us dream big and complete the corresponding daily, weekly, and monthly tasks to grow our business.

Reflect: ***When I set goals for myself, do I tend to under- or over-estimate what I can realistically achieve? If I were to create a vision board today, who or what are the people, things, and experiences that motivate me to work hard?***

Setting a sales goal and creating a vision board are practical ways to guide and motivate our work. If we tend to underestimate ourselves, let's think about having God-sized vision! If we tend to overestimate what we can handle, remember God wants us to also have balance and rest, and that there's more to life than sales. Hopefully we can find a balance somewhere between lacking faith in ourselves and God, and unrealistically stretching ourselves. Our goals should thoughtfully incorporate not just income needs and wants, but also our family and other commitments.

Reflect: *Do my other life priorities balance and fit with my real estate goals?*

> **Philippians 4:12-13 (NLT)**
>
> "I know how to live on almost nothing or with everything. I have learned the secret of living in every situation, whether it is with a full stomach or empty, with plenty or little. For I can do everything through Christ, who gives me strength."

Prayer prompt: *God, you know all my needs and wants; for example, I need __________ and I hope for __________. You are the source of my leads and opportunities. You know how many and which clients I will work with this year. I want your vision to become my vision. I trust in you that you will always provide. My career belongs to you! In Jesus' name, Amen.*

How much more powerful will our career goals be if we also align them with some life and spiritual goals? One way to make a spiritual goal is using Bible verses. I have a 'life' Bible verses and also a 'career' verse. I usually also choose a theme verse each year. These all serve as my compass for ministry in my daily life and work. Just as we reverse engineer our yearly sales goals to shape our daily, weekly, and monthly real estate tasks, our life and career Bible verses can shape and remind us of how we want to live and act each day.

When considering a life or career verse, think of one that's broad enough to resonate both now and into the future. A yearly or quarterly verse may have a narrower focus for a shorter-term spiritual goal. There are no rules! God will lead you to His right verse(s) for you and for this time.

Reflect: ***Do I have a favorite verse or two? Why are these my favorites? Are there any verses specific to my real estate career that encourage me?***

Your verses will be unique and special to you. Here are just a few examples of potential life and career verses; feel free to adopt them. Try looking up different Bible translations and paraphrases of the same verse until you find the wording that strikes just the right chord for you. This is an exercise that might take some time—have fun with it!

Matthew 6:33 (NLT)

"Seek the Kingdom of God above all else, and live righteously, and he will give you everything you need."

2 Corinthians 9:11 (NIV)

"You will be enriched in every way so that you can be generous on every occasion, and through us your generosity will result in thanksgiving to God."

Psalm 37:4 (NLT)

"Take delight in the LORD, and he will give you your heart's desires."

John 13:34-35 (AMP)

"I am giving you a new commandment, that you love one another. Just as I have loved you, so you too are to love one another. By this everyone will know that you are My disciples, if you have love and unselfish concern for one another."

Colossians 3:23-24 (NIV)

"Whatever you do, work at it with all your heart, as working for the Lord, not for human masters, since you know that you will receive an inheritance from the Lord as a reward. It is the Lord Christ you are serving."

Proverbs 11:25 (NIV)

"A generous person will prosper; whoever refreshes others will be refreshed."

Proverbs 3:5-6 (NIV)

"Trust in the LORD with all your heart
 and lean not on your own understanding;
in all your ways submit to him,
 and he will make your paths straight."

Once you choose your verse(s), look for artwork (or create your own!) featuring that verse. You could print it out, frame it, or include it on a vision board. Commit it to memory so you can be continuously inspired in your daily life and work. Regular reflection on these verses will help us keep God's vision, our vision.

Prayer prompt: *Lord, as I search the Bible for your words of encouragement and inspiration, please direct me to the verses that are a perfect fit for me. Let your vision for my career become my vision!*

Loving to learn

Rooms of treasure

When I first started in real estate, Jodee Farm, an agent I admire who has decades of experience in the business said: “I love this job because every day is different. Even after all these years, I still get to learn new things all the time!” I still remember the glow on her face and felt encouraged to hear this from such an experienced agent. I was too new to realize that in real estate, we are always in learning mode.

Reflect: ***What’s my general attitude about learning? Do I get excited about learning, or do I groan every time I have to attend a Continuing Education class?***

Proverbs 12:1 (MSG)

“If you love learning, you love the discipline that goes with it—how shortsighted to refuse correction!”

Proverbs 12:15 (AMP)

“The way of the [arrogant] fool [who rejects God’s wisdom] is right in his own eyes,
But a wise and prudent man is he who listens to counsel.”

Prayer prompt: ***Dear God, please give me a heart that’s humble and excited to learn. Thank you for your many proverbs and verses that teach about obtaining more wisdom.***

Ten years into my career (but for the first time), I started helping a buyer interested in a Hawaiian Homestead listing. These properties are leased only to Native Hawaiians, defined as someone with at least 50% Hawaiian blood. Eligible individuals must register to have their bloodlines vetted and are then placed on a very long waiting list. If a homestead property becomes available, they can make an offer.

In the few days my buyers and I had until the offer deadline, we embarked on a frenzied crash course on homestead properties. There were dozens of other eligible buyers interested, so I wanted to forecast the appraisal value as accurately as possible for our offer to be competitive. Since it was a leased home, I learned that appraisers do not use the normal comparable sales method to establish value. Instead, the replacement cost method based on current construction costs is the standard.

I vaguely remembered the replacement cost method from Pre-Licensing class but had never used it in practice. I scrambled to ask co-workers, lenders, and a staff member at the Department of Hawaiian Homelands for advice and recent examples. I felt like a brand-new agent: listening, taking lots of notes, and not assuming anything in order to serve and help my clients' best chances for this home. My clients and I were blessed that the knowledge we needed was freely shared when we sought it out. And God blessed them with the house!

There will never be a day in real estate where we can proclaim we finally know everything. Every day brings change: ups and downs in market conditions and interest rates, new laws, updated contract forms, different technology, and newly built neighborhoods or buildings. This is why we are required to take Continuing Education classes. Some might think the classes are a chore, but to be successful in this business for the long haul like Jodee, we should always be excited to "get to" learn!

What I enjoy most about taking classes is that I can meet and reconnect with peers. You just never know; there may be a God connection made while you are at class! I love this proverb that makes building a house a fitting analogy for learning:

Proverbs 24:3-4 (NIV)

"By wisdom a house is built,
  and through understanding it is established;
through knowledge its rooms are filled
  with rare and beautiful treasures."

Prayer prompt: *Dear Jesus, I want to love learning and love knowledge. Even after I've established my real estate career "house" from the proverb above, I want to continue to learn so I can fill each room with treasure. In Your name I pray, Amen.*

Working on Sundays

Making time for rest

Real estate never sleeps! We work weekdays when escrow, title, and lenders are working; then we work evenings and weekends when our clients are available. Sundays are one of the busier workdays since it's still the main day for public open houses. The Bible teaches about keeping the Sabbath holy and resting on the seventh day, so it's a valid question: is it godly to do our real estate work on Sundays?

Reflect: ***Do I intentionally set time aside each week to rest and honor the Lord? Do I have a hard time taking a break from work?***

Prayer prompt: ***Lord, I want to understand your Word and obey your teaching about keeping a day of rest. I want to honor you with my schedule and time. Please give me clarity and peace.***

Exodus 20:8-10 (AMP)

"Remember the Sabbath (seventh) day to keep it holy (set apart, dedicated to God). Six days you shall labor and do all your work, but the seventh day is a Sabbath [a day of rest dedicated] to the Lord your God; on that day you shall not do any work"

Genesis 2:1-3 (AMP)

"So the heavens and the earth were completed, and all their hosts (inhabitants). And by the seventh day God completed His work which He had done, and He rested (ceased) on the seventh day from all His work which He had done. So God blessed the seventh day and sanctified it [as His own, that is, set it apart as holy from other days], because in it He rested from all His work which He had created and done."

During creation, God worked diligently for six days and then rested on the seventh. Of course, God doesn't need rest to function well! But we humans have physical limits; God was modeling what hard work and rest look like. Then, in the fourth commandment, God reiterated the need to rest, and further defined the purpose of the seventh day: it is a holy day to honor Him. The origin of the word is the Hebrew word *sabat*, which means "to rest or stop or cease from work."

Since many pastors and clergy must preach and work on Sundays, they take Mondays or another day during the week as their Sabbath. Whatever day we deem our Sabbath, what is undeniable is God's command to take one day each week to rest and honor Him. In the following New Testament teaching, Jesus wants us to understand the 'why' behind the practice.

Romans 14:5-6 (AMP)

"One person regards one day as better [or more important] than another, while another regards every day [the same as any other]. Let everyone be fully convinced (assured, satisfied) in his own mind. He who observes the day, observes it for the Lord. He who eats, eats for the Lord, since he gives thanks to God; while he who abstains, abstains for the Lord and gives thanks to God."

Reflect: ***What does it mean to set aside a Sabbath day? Why is taking a Sabbath important to God? Is it also important to me and my family?***

Taking a true Sabbath is a challenge for many of us. We know it's important to give God a portion of our week, just as we give a portion of our income with our tithes. It's also important to take care of our physical and mental health—we are God's vessels. But at the same time, we want to be responsive to and available for our clients. A good friend and top agent, James Chan, shared:

> *I'm wired (it's a Chan family trait) to always keep moving and I hate to lose any work opportunity. But after 19 years and through many challenges in the business, God has delivered. I've learned the faithfulness of the Lord so I try to honor Him more now with my time.*

I know some agents who take Sundays off altogether and their business is still wildly blessed. We can gently explain to our clients that we take a certain day off every week. We can ask a co-worker or manager to be an emergency contact. We can "let go and let God" and not fret about non-emergencies that can wait. We can choose to obey and honor God.

This chapter is not about definitively telling you if it's right or wrong to work on Sundays. How you choose a Sabbath is a private decision between you and the Lord. You may seek input from your family, pastor, or clergy as you seek your personal answer. I pray that some of the verses and here will form a framework to guide you as you consider work and rest in light of God's commands.

Prayer prompt: *God, you created me for work, as well as for worship and rest. You command me to take a day to rest and I want to honor you. For me and my schedule, I plan to take my Sabbath on __________. Help me to communicate this well to my clients and colleagues. Help me to make this a regular and worshipful practice. In Jesus' name, Amen.*

When your pipeline is dry

Choose joy and give

Whenever there is a lull in our pipeline, it's only human to panic. No leads or escrows today means we won't have a closing or paycheck for at least a month or more. We check and double check our savings account and calculate how long we can get by.

Reflect: ***How am I feeling today about my business and finances? Have I ever had a similar rough patch before? What happened then?***

There is a famous passage by Jesus in Matthew 6 starting at verse 25 that is often quoted for lean times like this. It's comforting to read that God knows our needs and will provide. Here are the last few verses of the passage:

> **Matthew 6:31-34 (NLT)**
>
> "So don't worry about these things, saying, 'What will we eat? What will we drink? What will we wear?' These things dominate the thoughts of unbelievers, but your heavenly Father already knows all your needs. Seek the Kingdom of God above all else, and live righteously, and he will give you everything you need. So don't worry about tomorrow, for tomorrow will bring its own worries. Today's trouble is enough for today."

Prayer prompt: *God, stop my doubting and replace it with faith that you will provide for me. I want to give you all my worries and focus instead on seeking your Kingdom and living righteously. Help me know exactly how to do that today.*

Instead of worrying, let's follow Jesus and Matthew 6:33 and seek God first. Instead of anxiety, let's intentionally do some righteous living. There is always a God Layer on our lives even during times when our business is slow.

Let's change our focus away from our lack of clients and closings and flip the switch with an exercise in generosity. Let's replace our scarcity mindset with an abundance mindset; here are two Bible passages where there is a juxtaposition of lack and joy:

2 Corinthians 8:1-5 (NLT)

"Now I want you to know, dear brothers and sisters, what God in his kindness has done through the churches in Macedonia. They are being tested by many troubles, and they are very poor. But they are also filled with abundant joy, which has overflowed in rich generosity. For I can testify that they gave not only what they could afford, but far more. And they did it of their own free will. They begged us again and again for the privilege of sharing in the gift for the believers in Jerusalem. They even did more than we had hoped, for their first action was to give themselves to the Lord and to us, just as God wanted them to do."

Habakkuk 3:17-18 (NIV)

"Though the fig tree does not bud and there are no grapes on the vines, though the olive crop fails and the fields produce no food, though there are no sheep in the pen and no cattle in the stalls, yet I will rejoice in the Lord, I will be joyful in God my Savior."

Reflect: ***Can I be joyful like the Macedonians even during this time of lack? Can I be an exceptional giver? If not, why is it a challenge for me?***

I'm not suggesting here that you give money, although you may choose to do so if you hear God calling you to give a monetary offering. Instead, I want to suggest that we give away one of our precious possessions as a sacrificial offering to the Lord.

Look inside your closets and cupboards: what treasures do you have there? Is there an item that could fill another person's need or bring them joy? Although "one person's trash is another's treasure," for this exercise, let's try to find something we still find value and joy in, something it would pain us to give away.

Once you choose an item, next find someone to bless. God may bring to mind someone you know, but if not, you might try a "Buy Nothing" group. I joined my local Honolulu group; it's a worldwide movement. Members in the same area gift or ask for items and meet in person to exchange them—no money or barter changes hands. Post a photo and description of the item, field responses from interested people, choose someone, and arrange to meet in person for the exchange. As an option, you can state that there may be no reselling of your gifted item. I've found it's very satisfying to meet the random neighbors God calls on us to love. I've even posted a gift of "time and transport," where I offered to run an errand or delivery.

The following verse biblically supports the concept of these "Buy Nothing" groups:

> **2 Corinthians 8:14 (AMP)**
>
> "at this present time your surplus [over necessities] is going to supply their need, so that [at some other time] their surplus may be given to supply your need, that there may be equality"

Sometimes as agents, the way our incomes fluctuate can feel like a feast or famine roller coaster. The "Buy Nothing" concept of living in community is to give generously during times of plenty, and not be ashamed to ask and receive during our times of need. Today's faith exercise takes it deeper with a challenge to give joyfully during and despite our time of need. Showing faith in action is always pleasing to the Lord. I pray that He blesses you many times in return, in His miraculous time and loving way!

Prayer prompt: *Lord, I want to be joyful even during this slower time! I want to give sacrificially today: show me a specific person or place, and the specific gift you want me to give with joy. I want to give cheerfully, out of faith. I praise you and know you will take care of my pipeline. I'm confident that ____________. Thank you for ____________.*

When you're broke

Jehovah Jireh

The words, 'I'm broke,' are often said as an excuse or joke, even if we still have money in our bank account, a roof over our heads, and food on the table. If we find ourselves casually thinking, 'I'm broke' a lot, perhaps we need to shift from a 'glass half-empty' to a 'glass half-full' point of view. An easy way to start thinking glass half-full is by asking, 'How has God blessed me?'

Reflect: ***Am I good at counting my blessings? Where has The God Layer been active in my life recently? Make a gratitude list today of at least seven things.***

If you're in a season where you're having difficulty finding any blessings to count; if the glass isn't half full or empty, it's just plain empty, then keep reading.

One of the many names of God is "Jehovah-Jireh," which means "The Lord will provide." The reference comes from the book of Genesis chapter 22, when God tested Abraham's faith and loyalty: would Abraham obey and sacrifice his only precious son Isaac, the long-awaited child he and his wife Sarah had prayed and hoped for?

> **Genesis 22:1-3 (NIV)**
>
> "Some time later God tested Abraham. He said to him, 'Abraham!'

'Here I am,' he replied.

Then God said, 'Take your son, your only son, whom you love—Isaac—and go to the region of Moriah. Sacrifice him there as a burnt offering on a mountain I will show you.'

Early the next morning Abraham got up and loaded his donkey. He took with him two of his servants and his son Isaac. When he had cut enough wood for the burnt offering, he set out for the place God had told him about."

Between verses 1 and 2, Abraham must have had a sleepless night. Imagine his confusion and anxiety as he tried to be obedient to the Lord even while not understanding what would happen to his son Isaac.

We have sleepless nights when we are worried about our business. If God asked us to make a similarly huge sacrifice, would we have a trusting attitude like Abraham? Abraham didn't know what God was planning; we also don't know God's ways and plans with our income. God was testing Abraham's faith—as He tests ours to see if we are fully trusting in His provision.

Genesis 22:9-13 (NIV)

"When they reached the place God had told him about, Abraham built an altar there and arranged the wood on it. He bound his son Isaac and laid him on the altar, on top of the wood. Then he reached out his hand and took the knife to slay his son. But the angel of the Lord called out to him from heaven, 'Abraham! Abraham!'

'Here I am,' he replied.

'Do not lay a hand on the boy,' he said. 'Do not do anything to him. Now I know that you fear God, because you have not withheld from me your son, your only son.'

Abraham looked up and there in a thicket he saw a ram caught by its horns. He went over and took the ram and sacrificed it as a burnt offering instead of his son. So Abraham called that place The Lord Will Provide. And to this day it is said, 'On the mountain of the Lord it will be provided.'"

Abraham passed the test with devotion and faith, and he was rewarded: God provided a lamb to sacrifice instead of Isaac. So Abraham named this place Jehovah-Jireh: "The Lord will provide." Abraham must have felt so relieved once he passed God's test and understood God's plan.

Reflect: ***How is my faith doing these days? Would I offer my most precious thing or person to God as a sacrificial offering? Do I trust that God is my Jehovah-Jireh?***

Today, you are still in the dark about how The God Layer will play out in your current financial test. I pray you can trust God does have a plan. I challenge you now to prepare a sacrificial offering to show God you trust Him.

Luke 21:1-4 (NIV)

"As Jesus looked up, he saw the rich putting their gifts into the temple treasury. He also saw a poor widow put in two very small copper coins. 'Truly I tell you,' he said, 'this poor widow has put in more than all the others. All these people gave their gifts out of their wealth; but she out of her poverty put in all she had to live on.'"

This poor widow had a crazy faithful mindset! Instead of a broke mindset, she had a heart of worship. We don't know anything else about her; God wants us to learn from her attitude and this one faithful action. The story isn't just that she had great faith. The point is that she had great faith *and* she gave her two coins to the Lord.

God rewards faith, but He rewards faith in action even more. Because you have turned to this chapter and opened your Bible today, you have performed an act of faith. You have made a deposit into your heavenly treasure!

Prayer prompt: *Lord, I am also poor today, like the widow. Are you teaching me to have faith like hers, to give what I have, or both? Please give me courage to obey you as Abraham did. In Jesus' name, Amen.*

Action: *Reach out to a brother or sister in Christ whom you trust. Ask God to show you who; it doesn't necessarily need to be someone in real estate. Share your gratitude list, a little about your situation, and what God has taught you today. Share humbly and from your heart. Let your friend pray for you. If you can't think of anyone, please call me!*

When you have a free day

Divine appointments

One morning in 2021, God placed an idea about my career on my heart first thing in the morning. It was exciting and scary, and I wanted to talk it through with someone I trusted. I prayed and journaled a little, and then decided to reach out to my agent friend and mentor, Liz Garcia. I sent her a text first to ask if she had some time to chat. She immediately replied yes, and we were on the phone within a minute! It seemed almost too perfect that Liz should be available as soon as I needed to talk. Later, I found out her side of the story and knew then it was a 'divine appointment': a meeting or conversation that seems to happen by chance, but we know in our hearts that God planned it.

Liz had woken up that morning with no appointments. She spent time in prayer, then proclaimed to God that the rest of the day was His! She told God she would wait, open and available for Him to fill her schedule. Then she got my text! She immediately knew I was God's first assignment for her day.

I benefitted from the fact that Liz was already in the right godly mindset to give me advice just when I needed it. She was so selfless to give her free day over to the Lord's purposes—you can understand why I have Liz as my mentor. She was confident that God would put her to work that day—almost challenging Him to show up! If we follow her example, God will surely add an extra God Layer to our life. Let's invite Him to do good works through us for His purposes.

Ephesians 3:20 (TPT)

"Never doubt God's mighty power to work in you and accomplish all this. He will achieve infinitely more than your greatest request, your most unbelievable dream, and exceed your wildest imagination! He will outdo them all, for his miraculous power constantly energizes you."

Reflect: *What do I like to do whenever I have a free day? What do I think of Liz's example?*

Corrie Ten Boom, Nazi concentration camp survivor and author of *The Hiding Place*, wrote: "If the devil cannot make us bad, he'll make us busy." Unfortunately, the devil is just as capable of filling our schedule with meaningless, even harmful things. If we aren't on our guard, any spare time we happen to have might be stolen by the enemy.

1 Peter 5:8 (NLT)

"Stay alert! Watch out for your great enemy, the devil. He prowls around like a roaring lion, looking for someone to devour."

Deliberate acts like Liz's send an unequivocal message to the devil that says: 'This day belongs to God, so don't even bother encroaching on my schedule!'

God's divine appointments may not necessarily be to meet with someone. It could be a phone call like mine with Liz. It might be sending a card or text to a friend God puts on your heart. God may lead you to perform an act of service for someone. He will put an idea or a person in your head; however crazy it might seem, just go with it!

A few months after my divine appointment with Liz, I woke up to a day without appointments. I dedicated my free day to the Lord and He ended up filling it with writing the beginning of this chapter. In fact, God used many free days during the slower real estate market in late 2022 and 2023 for me to work on this book.

As I worked on this chapter, I searched for a fitting verse. Because God is faithful, He gave me this one:

> **Psalm 143:8 (NIV)**
>
> "Let the morning bring me word of your unfailing love,
> for I have put my trust in you.
> Show me the way I should go,
> for to you I entrust my life."

Did you wake up today with no appointments? What a blessing! Spend some quality time with the Lord and try offering up your day—or even just a part of it—to Him. Then wait expectantly to see what He plans for you!

Prayer prompt: ***Thank you, Lord, for this gift of a day with no appointments. I offer up my time to you; please bless me with a divine appointment or two! Prepare my heart to serve whomever and however you decide. I'm excited to see what you have planned!***

When you're crazy busy

The most important appointment each day

The first thing many of us do upon waking is check our phone for emails and texts that came in overnight. All day and into the evening, we rush to appointments and catch up on paperwork that's piling up. Everyone seems to want a piece of our day—and that's not even counting our family and other commitments.

Reflect: ***What are the signs for me that work is getting too busy? When my work is crazy busy, how does it affect me and my relationships?***

Taking a Sabbath once a week is the subject of a previous chapter. Whatever day we choose as our rest day, the main thing is to have one and plan for it. We should also take a daily pause for the most important appointment of each day: time with the Lord.

> **Mark 1:35 (NIV)**
>
> "Very early in the morning, while it was still dark, Jesus got up, left the house and went off to a solitary place, where he prayed."

Reflect: ***How would I grade my consistency (A through F) in having daily 'quiet time' with God? What are the reasons I am not more consistent?***

Prayer prompt: ***Jesus, I want to follow your example and make time to pray to our Father. Help me to __________.***

Spending time with God daily is as vital to our spiritual health as drinking water is to our physical health. When we pray, read, and meditate on God's Word, we drink from His living water. If we don't refill our spiritual tanks, God's blessing on our lives and businesses will dry up.

Indeed, we are so busy because God has blessed us with all this business! When it rains, it pours! Thank you, Jesus! When was the last time we thanked God for blessing us so abundantly? Have we been too busy working to stop and give Him the glory due to Him?

Deuteronomy 8:11-14 (MSG)

"Make sure you don't forget God, your God, by not keeping his commandments, his rules and regulations that I command you today. Make sure that when you eat and are satisfied, build pleasant houses and settle in, see your herds and flocks flourish and more and more money come in, watch your standard of living going up and up—make sure you don't become so full of yourself and your things that you forget God"

Are we like the Israelites, who were prone to forget God's great provision and deliverance out of Egypt? I need this reminder all the time because I have a selfish habit of taking all the credit. When our business is thriving, let's not let it go to our heads.

A good loan officer friend of mine, Tim O'Leary, blocks off his schedule every day at 10:00am and 3:00pm:

> *It's only for a short pause, to thank and honor God. I find that it keeps me from going down a slippery slope. I feel refreshed and alive. Sometimes it's as short as me saying aloud to myself, 'Thank you, Jesus!'*

God will honor any and all time we prioritize Him. So even if it's just a few minutes like Tim, or if we intentionally wake up early and ignore messages and emails until after we've spent some time with the Lord, hold some time sacred—especially on the busiest days. Actually, you have already done so today by turning to this chapter; praise God! I pray that on the days we are blessed to work overtime, we make time with Jesus so that we won't become parched; so we can refill ourselves with His fresh living water.

> **John 4:13-14 (NLT)**
>
> "Jesus replied, 'Anyone who drinks this water will soon become thirsty again. But those who drink the water I give will never be thirsty again. It becomes a fresh, bubbling spring within them, giving them eternal life.'"

Prayer prompt: *Lord, thank you for __________. My cup overflows, and it's because __________. I want to give you all the glory for providing all this business!*

When you just got paid

Bursting barns and storehouses

The irregularity and uncertainty of being paid on commission truly builds our faith. We can spend months and even years serving a client for one well-earned payday. You've probably been anticipating this paycheck since the day you opened escrow, maybe even earlier. Especially if the journey before and during escrow has been a long one, now it's time to give thanks for the fruits of your labor!

Reflect: ***How long have I worked for this paycheck? What have I learned during this time? How has The God Layer been upon this transaction?***

Prayer prompt: ***Lord, thank you for providing this client, this transaction, and this paycheck. I recognize that all of it is your blessing. Help me to remember that you are Jehovah Jireh, my provider!***

Proverbs 3:9-10 (MSG)

"Honor God with everything you own;
give him the first and the best.
Your barns will burst,
your wine vats will brim over.""

Tithing is giving back the first portion—ten percent—of our paycheck to the Lord. God rewards us when we are obedient in tithing. It's an act of worship, as we give God the glory and recognition that He is our provider.

Reflect: *How do I feel about tithing?*

I learned the discipline—and blessings—of tithing from watching my father. Every single Sunday at church, he would get his checkbook out—even during the lowest point in our family's finances. This came during my high school years when his company went through a bankruptcy. For many months, I watched my mother figure out which bill to pay and in what order based on urgency.

Still, God always provided everything we needed, and even some non-essentials—like my shoes, gloves, and costume jewelry for my senior prom outfit. (I was blessed throughout my childhood that my godmother, Fumi, was an excellent seamstress—she designed and gifted me my prom dress!) I thank God for my father's commitment to tithing because other than that low point, our family was always blessed to overflowing. My father's weekly offering check modeled for me that he was recognizing God's provision for our family.

As an adult, I have not always been consistent with tithing. During my twenties and thirties, I fell away from the Lord. I had well-paying jobs in hotel and retail management and, I don't know why, but God still graciously blessed me even though I was not in relationship with Him. When I came back to my faith at age 40, I dedicated my brand-new real estate career to God, including a commitment to tithe no matter what. Even during those first few years when I had yet to build a consistent clientele, God provided—miraculously sometimes—a steady stream of clients and business. Hallelujah.

God will provide—to the point of overflowing! Here is one more passage where God challenges the Israelites (and us):

Malachi 3:8-12 (NIV)

"'Will a mere mortal rob God? Yet you rob me.

'But you ask, 'How are we robbing you?''

> ‘In tithes and offerings. You are under a curse—your whole nation—because you are robbing me. Bring the whole tithe into the storehouse, that there may be food in my house. Test me in this,’ says the Lord Almighty, ‘and see if I will not throw open the floodgates of heaven and pour out so much blessing that there will not be room enough to store it. I will prevent pests from devouring your crops, and the vines in your fields will not drop their fruit before it is ripe,’ says the Lord Almighty. ‘Then all the nations will call you blessed, for yours will be a delightful land,’ says the Lord Almighty.”

The first part of this passage sounds harsh. The latter part promises that God will pour out so much blessing on us—and He challenges us to test Him. Who wouldn’t want to be on the right side of this!? Amel Dominguez, a pastor friend and client, frames tithing in this enlightening way:

> *Would I rather have 100% of unblessed income, or 90% that has God’s blessing?*

Tithing is not a popular subject, but I know that God commands it and I feel He wants it mentioned here. As with any spiritual discipline, it takes practice. We may not be good at tithing right now, even though we understand God’s command and promise. Wherever you are in your faith and however you feel about tithing, I pray God will work in your heart today.

Prayer prompt: ***Dear Lord, thank you for your teaching and promises about tithing. I feel __________ about tithing because __________. I claim your promise that you will provide for me—to overflowing! Please increase my faith. Show me I can tithe from my paycheck today. I trust that you will bless me with even more transactions. In Jesus’ name, Amen.***

When you just got paid more than you need

Sowing into God's Kingdom

Getting a whale of a paycheck can feel like winning the lottery! Once we've tithed (see previous chapter), paid our bills, and saved for taxes and retirement, how are we spending any excess? When we find ourselves earning above and beyond what we need, it's tempting and totally human to want to treat ourselves with something special.

Reflect: ***Have I ever "blown" a big paycheck? What did I spend the money on? In hindsight, did I get a good return on my investment?***

Probably because He knew this topic is a human stressor and fixation, God wisely included many verses about money in the Bible. Pastor Rick Warren of Saddleback Church teaches that God gives us money to be used, not loved. One of his messages teaches how we can "diversify God's wealth" with five types of giving:

1. The Treasury Fund – This is our 10% tithe to our local church, which shows our worship and thanks to God for providing for us.

2. The Mutual Fund – This is money to love on others in the family of God when they have a need, or to encourage them with a gift or shared meal.

3. The Growth Fund – This is money invested in our own personal growth—classes, retreats, and books that feed our soul.

4. The Equity/Service Fund – This is money donated to people in need:

the poor and the homeless, for example.

5. The Global Fund – This is money given toward spreading the Good News of Jesus to unreached people.

Tithing—the first type of giving—is non-negotiable to the Lord. Pastor Rick's four other types might be considered optional, but there are many Bible verses about giving, especially type 2 (sharing with our brothers and sisters), and type 4 (giving to the poor). It's clear that God wants us to be generous above and beyond our tithes.

Romans 12:13 (NIV) – Type 2

"Share with the Lord's people who are in need. Practice hospitality."

Acts 4:32-35 (NIV) – Type 2

"All the believers were one in heart and mind. No one claimed that any of their possessions was their own, but they shared everything they had. With great power the apostles continued to testify to the resurrection of the Lord Jesus. And God's grace was so powerfully at work in them all that there were no needy persons among them. For from time to time those who owned land or houses sold them, brought the money from the sales and put it at the apostles' feet, and it was distributed to anyone who had need."

Proverbs 19:17 (NIV) – Type 4

"Whoever is kind to the poor lends to the LORD, and he will reward them for what they have done."

Luke 12:33-34 (MSG) – Type 4

"'Be generous. Give to the poor. Get yourselves a bank that can't go bankrupt, a bank in heaven far from bankrobbers, safe from embezzlers, a bank you can bank on. It's obvious, isn't it? The place where your treasure is, is the place you will most want to be, and end up being.'"

Reflect: ***How does my heart respond to these verses about giving? Why has God given me more than enough today?***

If you have been faithfully tithing, I pray you will consider (or continue) to joyfully give above and beyond! I add the word "joyfully" because God doesn't want anything given out of duty or with resentment:

2 Corinthians 9:6-9 (NIV)

"Remember this: Whoever sows sparingly will also reap sparingly, and whoever sows generously will also reap generously. Each of you should give what you have decided in your heart to give, not reluctantly or under compulsion, for God loves a cheerful giver. And God is able to bless you abundantly, so that in all things at all times, having all that you need, you will abound in every good work. As it is written:

'They have freely scattered their gifts to the poor;
their righteousness endures forever.'"

If you were just blessed with a big paycheck, how might you spend some of it to further the Lord's kingdom around you? Here is a story that might inspire you:

Morris Takushi is an amazing man of God I am blessed to know. He continues his construction and renovation business even at 84 years young. In July 2023, he invited me for lunch and a tour of his most recent project. He and his crew had done many renovations around his church, Nuuanu Baptist in Honolulu: a spacious and organized new kitchen, perfect for cooking for large groups; a nursing mothers' room with comfortable chairs, a crib, and a large TV hooked up to view the worship service; and inviting new offices and classrooms.

At a sizable cost for materials and labor, Morris donated the entire project. The day of my visit, the church had throngs of children attending summer Vacation Bible School, and the spiritual energy was alive! Morris told me the original core congregation has been aging and going to heaven, but God had used their online ministry during the COVID pandemic to bring new young families from the neighborhood. Morris' gift is already giving a tangible return on investment—and will continue to for decades to come.

The word 'extravagant' contains the word 'extra'. Morris gave extravagantly based on his means and his love for God. Today, God has given you extra with a large paycheck. What God Layers, what blessings, could be activated as part of this check? Giving to the Lord will have eternal returns!

Prayer prompt: *Dear God, thank you for your continuous blessings with this very large paycheck. Thank you for __________. Please give me an idea where I can invest in your kingdom. Please teach me how to be a good steward of what you've given me, and how to give extravagantly.*

When you have continuous success and income

Blessed to be a blessing

If you're blessed to find you're no longer struggling or worrying about having enough income, hallelujah! When God blesses our business abundantly and continuously, our paychecks may increase, but so may our egos. Let's be on guard: Satan will try to bait us into thinking we've achieved all this success ourselves.

> **Deuteronomy 8:17-18 (MSG)**
>
> "If you start thinking to yourselves, 'I did all this. And all by myself. I'm rich. It's all mine!'—well, think again. Remember that GOD, your God, gave you the strength to produce all this wealth"

Reflect: ***Have I changed with my increased career success and income? What are some new temptations I'm facing?***

If we have been good stewards with a little, God may be trusting us with even more—not for ourselves, but for us to steward on His behalf. Let's remain humble and continue to give God the credit and glory for all He's providing. Let's continue to give back and worship Him with our tithes from every paycheck.

Prayer prompt: *Lord, I come before you with my head bowed and a humble heart. For whatever reason, you have chosen to shower me with so much business and income; I want to continue to trust in you. Thank you for __________ and __________.*

Another way the enemy may try to tempt us is with 'lifestyle bloat': as we earn more, we tend to spend more on the finer things this world offers. On God's eternal timeline, these things will decay. Still, I am guilty of rationalizing that I deserve to treat myself to that designer handbag or luxury car.

Pastor Jordan Seng of Bluewater Mission and author of *Miracle Work: A Down-to-Earth Guide to Supernatural Ministries* taught the analogy that having a lot of money is like eating a lot of calories: eating more calories than we burn is harmful to our health; it leads to the sin of gluttony. But if we use and have a purpose for every calorie, we can keep eating. Olympic swimmer Michael Phelps famously consumed 10,000 calories a day while training; he used all those calories for gain—and for gold!

Like excess calories, excess money can harm our spiritual health. Excess money spent frivolously leads to the sin of materialism. The Bible warns against the love of money, the "root of all evil" (1 Timothy 6:10).

Reflect: *What are some possible reasons God has blessed my business? Am I being a good steward of the Lord's money?*

If God blesses us with a lot of money, of course He wants us to have a good life. But once we have what we need to be comfortable, He's entrusting the rest to us to invest for His good. As we learned in the last chapter, giving to others reaps an eternal return on investment. Another reason is that when we give to others, their hearts become open to the Lord.

2 Corinthians 9:10-15 (NLT)

"For God is the one who provides seed for the farmer and then bread to eat. In the same way, he will provide and increase your resources and then produce a great harvest of generosity in you.

Yes, you will be enriched in every way so that you can always be generous. And when we take your gifts to those who need them, they will thank God. So two good things will result from this ministry of giving—the needs of the believers in Jerusalem will be met, and they will joyfully express their thanks to God.

As a result of your ministry, they will give glory to God. For your generosity to them and to all believers will prove that you are obedient to the Good News of Christ. And they will pray for you with deep affection because of the overflowing grace God has given to you. Thank God for this gift too wonderful for words!"

Verse 11 (underlined above) is one of my career verses. God showed me this verse my first month in the real estate business (March 2012). I drew this diagram:

The reason God is blessing you with continuous success and pay is so you can be a blessing on His behalf.

Prayer prompt: *Lord, I see that I am 'blessed to be a blessing.' Please show me who I can bless. I want to see others give you praise because of your gifts through me. I give you all the glory for gifting me with the ability to serve you well in real estate. Help me understand why you are entrusting me with excess income. I want to store up eternal treasure according to your will. In Jesus' name, Amen.*

Chapter 5 earlier in this section covers the polar opposite situation—"When you're broke." If you are reading today's chapter about your business and income overflowing, it's probably been a while since you were broke. But there is probably an agent you know who is broke and crying out to the Lord in faith. Who comes to mind? Take some time to pray and ask God for instructions.

Luke 6:34-36 (TPT)

"'If you lend money only to those you know will repay you, what credit is that to your character? Even those who don't know God do that. Rather love your enemies and continue to treat them well. When you lend money, don't despair if you are never paid back, for it is not lost. You will receive a rich reward and you will be known as true children of the Most High God, having his same nature. Be like your Father who is famous for his kindness to heal even the thankless and cruel. Overflow with mercy and compassion for others, just as your heavenly Father overflows with mercy and compassion for all.'"

Action: *Go to the person God has shown you. Speak to them using whatever words God gives you. Let the Lord guide you to do whatever is needed to bless them—and be sure to explain that this is not a loan. Share 2 Corinthians 9:11 with them as your motivation. Maybe there is a God Layer in this connection!*

I want to give my life to Jesus

It's time!

Thank you for turning to this chapter! God planned for you to read it today—it's time! God loves you so much, and He is ready to envelop you in His arms. As you say the prayer in this chapter, you will be filled with the Holy Spirit. This most important decision to dedicate your life to God will change you from the inside out!

Revelation 21 and 22 are the very last chapters of not only the book of Revelation, but the entire Bible. They are an uplifting grand finale of the greatest book of all time. Anytime I feel down, hopeless, or unloved, reading these chapters completely alters my mood and perspective. You can turn to the end of a physical Bible, download a Bible app, or just search for Revelation 21 and 22 on the web; please take some time now and read. You'll be reading a vision God gave John; it's about the future of heaven and earth.

Here are a few of the key verses:

Revelation 21:5-7 (NIV)

"He who was seated on the throne [God] said, 'I am making everything new!' Then he said, 'Write this down, for these words are trustworthy and true.'

He said to me: 'It is done. I am the Alpha and the Omega, the Beginning and the End. To the thirsty I will give water with

> out cost from the spring of the water of life. Those who are victorious will inherit all this, and I will be their God and they will be my children.'"

No matter your situation in life, recognizing there is a God Layer on it will infinitely improve it. We are victorious because we are adopted into God's family.

> **Revelation 22:14 (NLT)**
>
> "Blessed are those who wash their robes. They will be permitted to enter through the gates of the city and eat the fruit from the tree of life."

Here is a simplified explanation of how we have eternal life in heaven by believing in Jesus:

- Anyone who is a sinner (that's every single one of us) was destined to spend eternity in hell without Jesus.
- When Jesus came to the earth, He was God in human form, pure and sinless. His mission was to die on the cross and take all of humanity's sins upon His unblemished self. In our place, He went to hell for three days.
- Then God raised Jesus from the dead. There are many human accounts of people who saw Jesus die on the cross, then walk and talk a few days later.
- Because Jesus went to hell on our behalf, when we die our physical death, we will join Him in heaven.

Your name has always been written in God's "Book of Life." You just need to acknowledge that you believe Jesus died for your sins by praying this simple prayer:

Prayer prompt: *Dear Jesus, I believe you can take who I am and how I feel today and make me new. I want to drink your water of life; I am so thirsty.*

Anything bad in my life—my sin—is the result of how all humans were separated from you. But today I give you my heart. I ask you to forgive my sins and "wash my robes."

Jesus, I cry out your name. I acknowledge you as my Lord and Savior. I believe you died on the cross for my sins. Your death on the cross redeems me, so I can enter heaven. Thank you.

Please teach me how to follow you for my remaining days. Give me your guidance in my real estate career and every facet of my life. I can't wait to spend eternity with you!

In your precious name, Jesus, I pray. Amen.

By praying this prayer, you have joined the family of believers! Can you feel the hope and peace of Jesus!? Here are a few more Bible verses for encouragement and confirmation that your life has been forever changed:

John 14:6 (NLT)

"Jesus told him, 'I am the way, the truth, and the life. No one can come to the Father except through me.'"

John 3:16-17 (NLT)

"For this is how God loved the world: He gave his one and only Son, so that everyone who believes in him will not perish but have eternal life. God sent his Son into the world not to judge the world, but to save the world through him."

Luke 15:10 (NIV)

"In the same way, I tell you, there is rejoicing in the presence of the angels of God over one sinner who repents."

I praise God for you! Everyone in heaven is having a party for you!

Action: ***Is there anyone who played a part in sharing Jesus with you? There may be several people throughout your life. Call them and let them know you prayed to accept Jesus today! If you can't think of anyone, I would love to hear from you!***

I'm ready to come back to Jesus

The recklessly extravagant grace of God

The title of this chapter assumes you gave your life to Jesus before, but maybe you've drifted away from Him. If you've never entrusted your life to Jesus, you can also read the chapter just before this one.

I grew up going to church, and as a teenager I committed my life to Jesus and was baptized. Then I lost my way during my twenties and thirties—but my faithful parents never stopped praying for me. In my late thirties, I was an executive for a small jewelry chain—materially rich but spiritually anemic. As I approached my fortieth birthday, I went through an existential mid-life crisis: what was the purpose of my life? I felt empty, and that I hadn't accomplished anything truly meaningful in 40 years.

God showed up (well, He had never left my side), and welcomed me back. I recommitted my life to Him, quit that job, and spent most of 2011 volunteering (that's the subject of another book). In 2012, God led me to a career in real estate, and it's become my place of ministry and purpose.

We all have ebbs and flows in our faith journey. God knows the details of your falling away and coming back to Him. What matters most is you're here now in response to a nudge from the Holy Spirit; hallelujah! Like the prodigal son's father in Luke chapter 15, God is always waiting for us to return to Him. He is ready for you today!

Luke 15:20-24 (NIV)

"So he got up and went to his father.

'But while he was still a long way off, his father saw him and was filled with compassion for him; he ran to his son, threw his arms around him and kissed him.

'The son said to him, 'Father, I have sinned against heaven and against you. I am no longer worthy to be called your son."

'But the father said to his servants, 'Quick! Bring the best robe and put it on him. Put a ring on his finger and sandals on his feet. Bring the fattened calf and kill it. Let's have a feast and celebrate. For this son of mine was dead and is alive again; he was lost and is found.' So they began to celebrate."

Timothy Keller wrote many excellent books on Christian living, including one titled *The Prodigal God*. The word "prodigal" means "recklessly extravagant." Keller flips our perspective on who is the prodigal: we usually think it's the younger son, who recklessly spent his inheritance. But I was enlightened to learn from Keller that the recklessly extravagant one is the father. The father's (and our Father God's) actions show his (His) extravagant and unconditional grace. This parable has always given me reassurance that God is waiting to welcome us back.

Luke 12:6-7 (TPT)

"'What is the value of your soul to God? Could your worth be defined by an amount of money? God doesn't abandon or forget even the small sparrow he has made. How then could he forget or abandon you? What about the seemingly minor issues of your life? Do they matter to God? Of course they do! So you never need to worry, for you are more valuable to God than anything else in this world.'"

Here are a few prayer prompts for us as we seek Him again today:

Prayer prompt: *Jesus, thank you for waiting patiently for me. As you know, I've been caught up with other 'idols' like __________. So first, I would like to confess my sins to you, and ask for your forgiveness.*

Next, I want to praise and thank you for your never-ending and recklessly extravagant love... Thank you for __________. I praise you for __________.

Jesus, this is where I am today...

I rededicate not only my life but also my real estate work to you. You've placed me in this business, among my clients and industry associates, for a higher purpose. Please help me look to you daily for your guidance and help. In your name, Amen.

One of God's missions with this book was to include this chapter. I am so excited about your renewed faith and trust in God today! May God use His Word to inspire you on your journey to see The God Layer upon your life and work. God will work through you as His light in the industry!

Reflect: *What opportunities is God giving me today to shine His light in my business?*

Philippians 1:6 (TPT)

"I pray with great faith for you, because I'm fully convinced that the One who began this gracious work in you will faithfully continue the process of maturing you until the unveiling of our Lord Jesus Christ!"

I encourage you to reach out to at least one brother or sister in Christ to share with them! I would also love to hear your testimony and how you see The God Layer at work in your life. I pray you continue to grow stronger in Jesus and in your faith.

Action: *Share with someone about your decision today. Ask them to pray with you. If you can't think of anyone, please call or email me!*

Meeting new clients

God's gifts

I had a 'come back to Jesus' experience at age 40, then started in real estate at 41. This career was the first time I dedicated my work to the Lord. Good thing, too—I really don't know how anyone can do this job without faith!

Reflect: ***How does my real estate work require faith in the Lord?***

Like most new agents, I struggled to find clients. Besides trying to reach out to everyone I knew, I sat open houses, door knocked, and sent farming postcards. God always graced me with clients just in time.

My first two clients were friends willing to take a chance on me. My third client came to an open house in search of a listing agent. It was my broker's listing and she asked me to come and see her home once I had finished the open house. I eventually helped her sell two homes! I did not do anything special to earn her business—I was an absolute beginner. I had been praying for God to send me a client, and it was very clear that He answered and provided.

If all we do is sit at home and pray for God to send us new clients, He might occasionally drop a client into our laps just like that, because He can. But the Bible says we can't be lazy and expect God to do all the work for us. We must do our part in the work, then He will bless our work.

Colossians 3:23 (NIV)

"Whatever you do, work at it with all your heart, as working for the Lord, not for human masters."

Psalm 90:17 (AMP)

"And let the [gracious] favor of the Lord our God be on us;
Confirm for us the work of our hands—
Yes, confirm the work of our hands."

Reflect: *Who were my first few clients, and how did I meet them? How am I working diligently to meet new clients?*

Five years into my career, I started working at a company whose website was a powerful lead generator. An algorithm (which always seemed random to us agents) assigned us new clients to serve. One day, the system scheduled me for a showing in Hawaii Kai. I didn't know anything about the buy until we met at the listing—the whole family showed up on a weekday morning. I was curious about why the school-aged kids were there since it wasn't a holiday. As we continued to talk, I found out the mother homeschooled the four children. I began to ask more questions about their needs and wants for their new home. Besides a dedicated space for a home classroom, they mentioned they had small to large groups of people over almost daily.

I was thinking to myself that the only families I knew who homeschooled their kids were Christians. I started hearing God's still, small voice. Emboldened by the Holy Spirit, I asked: "Are you folks Christians?"

They were! In fact, the father was a pastor at the church down the road. I was so excited to tell them I too was a Christian. The God Layer—our connection—was so clear to us all, and we bonded instantly. God wanted me to know that although outwardly the company system was assigning me leads, He is still the one in control over whom He sends to me!

John 1:16 (AMP)

"For out of His fullness [the superabundance of His grace and truth] we have all received grace upon grace [spiritual blessing upon spiritual blessing, favor upon favor, and gift heaped upon gift]."

Prayer prompt: *God, you are the giver of many blessings, favors, and gifts! Thank you for your latest blessings of my newest clients __________, and __________. No matter how it seems I connected with them, I know that ultimately, you gave them to me!*

Once God connects us with a new client, we must continue to work hard to serve them—as for the Lord. God never does anything without a higher purpose. As we give Him thanks for the new relationship, let's ask Him, 'Why have you sent me this client, Lord?'

God's reason might simply be to help them in real estate using Christ-like words and actions. But there might be other reasons God has up His sleeve! We might find out why at the first meeting, during the transaction, or after closing. Even if we never find out why God made our paths cross, we can still be aware that He is at work in this client. We get to partner with God as He works through us; what an honor that He uses us!

Incidentally, remember my earlier story of that open house I sat for my broker at the beginning of my career? Even though the seller, Jane, was my broker's longtime client, she and I became friends and have kept in touch over the years. This kind of meeting and relationship are also gifts from the Lord, even when they don't result in a transaction.

Prayer prompt: *Dear Lord, all good things—and clients—come from you! I praise you! Please help me to recognize you are behind every new client you bring me. Please guide me as I start each client relationship. Please show me your will for the clients I'm currently helping, and guide me with your still, small voice. In Jesus' name, Amen.*

When a family member or friend hires you

Building on an existing foundation

Throughout our careers, God will give us opportunities to serve our family and friends in real estate matters. They are often the ones who give us our first shot as new agents. We must cherish and honor these opportunities to serve them. As with any other client the Lord puts in our path, we can seek out His purpose for us as we serve our loved ones.

Reflect: ***What is my relationship history with this family member or friend? How have the dynamics of our relationship looked in the past? How might the dynamic need to shift as I serve them in real estate?***

These relationships usually pre-date our real estate career. If we are helping an uncle or grandparent who watched us grow up, they may still think of us as a child. A high school classmate might have trouble taking us seriously as a businessperson. We might find ourselves capitulating more to family and friends than we would to other clients when they want to lowball an offer or list at a higher price. Being assertive while remaining respectful is a balancing act. We may need to gently adjust the relationship's dynamic as we lead them in real estate.

Despite these challenges, there are blessings and potential God Layer opportunities to build on the existing relationship. Just as our friends and family will start to see us in a new way, we may discover their experience and insight. They may reveal stories and parts of their histories we never knew about. They may also point out our faults and weaknesses in a way other clients wouldn't. Let's remain open to their wisdom and input.

Proverbs 27:6 (AMP)

"Faithful are the wounds of a friend [who corrects out of love and concern]"

If you and your family member or friend have a foundation of good times and memories, that bond will help during the transaction. One of my first clients was my former boss, Bob Taylor. He was a CEO and former CFO and had also held a real estate license. He was already an expert at gently coaching me, so I continued to learn as I served him and his wife in a couple of transactions. It was comforting to know they already loved and trusted me.

But when we don't have a particularly good history with the family member or friend, let's look to the Lord with hopeful anticipation; we can pray this real estate connection becomes a turning point in our relationship. Even if they wronged us in the past or there's a longstanding grudge, they somehow still came to us for real estate help. This could become an important time for healing. If we show them love, God will use it for the good. In fact, this may be just the reason for this transaction—let's continue to look out for the presence of The God Layer.

1 Peter 4:8 (MSG)

"Most of all, love each other as if your life depended on it. Love makes up for practically anything."

Reflect: *Do I give this family or friend the same level of service as my other clients? Am I more—or less—patient and kind with my communication?*

We should begin a transaction with the future in mind. Our relationships with family and friends will continue beyond closing the transaction–hopefully stronger and closer than ever. God placed them in our lives for real estate for the near-term; how we handle this transaction will shape our continued relationship with them in the future–even into eternity.

> **2 Timothy 1:7 (AMP)**
>
> "For God did not give us a spirit of timidity or cowardice or fear, but [He has given us a spirit] of power and of love and of sound judgment and personal discipline [abilities that result in a calm, well-balanced mind and self-control]."

In this verse, Paul encourages Timothy to be bold when telling people about Jesus. I love the combination of words in this verse: power, love, sound judgement, personal discipline–all the ingredients for good communication with all our clients, but especially family and friend clients. Even during a delicate transaction with friends or family, I pray we can find our confidence and purpose in the Lord.

Reflect: *How might God use this transaction for the good? How can I work together with God?*

Prayer prompt: *Dear Jesus, thank you for allowing me to help __________ in real estate. I feel __________ and __________. It feels like a new facet of our relationship is being carved out, including how we communicate. I ask for your help as I handle the business transaction while showing your unconditional love.*

When you receive a referral

God loves to connect people

For many agents, referrals are the lifeblood of our business. It is truly an honor to receive one. When a friend or past client refers us, it means they think highly enough of us to recommend us to a friend or family member. It means we met or exceeded their expectations, and they are proud to be associated with us.

> **Proverbs 27:9 (TPT)**
>
> "Sweet friendships refresh the soul and awaken our hearts with joy, for good friends are like the anointing oil that yields the fragrant incense of God's presence."

Reflect: ***How do I know the referrer? How has God been at work in our relationship?***

The God Layer can be easy to see when God creates a new triangle of connection between you, the referrer, and the new client. Your relationship with the referrer will grow in new ways as you start a relationship with their friend or family member. Let's strive to exceed our referrer's and new client's expectations. If we dedicate the referral connection triangle and real estate work to the Lord, He will bless it.

Prayer prompt: ***Thank you, Lord, for giving me this new client ___________. More importantly, thank you for ____________, the referrer who connected us because of their trust in me. Please help me to honor them both. I understand I have a duty to serve them both as I also serve you with my work.***

We can keep the referrer lightly updated as we work with the new client. I say "lightly" because we must honor our new client's privacy and confidentiality. Let's have wisdom and be judicious about what details–if any–we share. If the referrer persists in asking for details, we can make a general comment about how it's going and thank them again for the referral.

Sometimes no transaction materializes with the new client–or perhaps not immediately. We can let the referrer know that real estate transactions can take months or years to come to fruition. Perhaps God has a reason He wants us to walk awhile with both the referrer and the new client.

If something goes awry with the referred client, out of courtesy to the referrer we can explain–maybe without all the gory details. I had a worst-case scenario where, after initially winning the listing, I had to fire a seller who was being uncooperative and combative. When I explained the break to the referrer friend, I took the blame for it not being a good fit. Thankfully, he was understanding. This doesn't have to be a totally squandered opportunity: we can ask the Lord what His purpose is, even when a connection has failed. It may have been to solidify our relationship with the referrer friend and not necessarily the new client.

The ultimate reason God might bless us with a piece of referral business is to bring either the referrer or the new client closer to Him! Perhaps the referrer is another Christian who has been witnessing to this new client–as we spend time with them, we can be an additional witness and voice for Christ. Or the opposite: I've had past friends who are non-believers refer me to new clients who turned out to be believers. When the new client and I discovered we are one in Christ, we began to pray together for our mutual friend. God is the Great Connector!

Ephesians 2:10 (NIV)

"For we are God's handiwork, created in Christ Jesus to do good works, which God prepared in advance for us to do."

Prayer prompt: *Father God, you are truly amazing in your plan and purpose–there are no accidental meetings. Thank you for __________. Please use this connection for your glory!*

When your client has an impossible situation

Never underestimate God

There are easy sales and difficult ones, and then there are impossible sales. Like all trials God gives us in life, I believe He gives us these impossible sales to grow our faith and show His almighty power. Even if our professional, human mind tells us to run away from an impossible sale, remember we have a God who loves impossible.

> **Matthew 19:26 (MSG)**
>
> "Jesus looked hard at them and said, 'No chance at all if you think you can pull it off yourself. Every chance in the world if you trust God to do it.'"

Reflect: ***When I face an impossible situation, what are my usual first reactions?***

One of my impossible sales involved helping the owner of a leasehold condo. In Hawaii, the owner of a leasehold property owns the unit/improvement but leases the land on which it stands separately. My seller wanted to sell their leasehold unit, and the landowner–a Christian organization–had also listed the land portion for sale. The potential buyer of my seller's unit could take full 'fee simple' ownership by buying both.

The landowner's price was high and non-negotiable, so to determine the leasehold unit's market value, we had to back out the land price from the comps. At best, with an impossibly high offer, the sellers might be able to break even. With a lower offer, they would have to bring cash to the closing table.

The seller had already met with a handful of agents who all turned down this impossible listing. He requested a listing consultation with me through my company's website. As I prepared the market analysis, I came to the same conclusion. I asked my husband (who is also an agent) to look at it; he said it would be a miracle sale. I felt defeated and questioned God: "Why did you bring this seller to me?"

I was tempted to cancel the consult, but I went to the initial meeting with plans to tell the seller his situation looked bleak. I discovered he was the son of a pastor. His faith had weakened (as happens to all of us), and he was resentful that his pleas to the Christian landowner had fallen on deaf ears. I marveled at how he bared his emotions (that was the work of the Holy Spirit) and I felt his profound pain.

I was unsure what to do or say. It was a rare opportunity for me to seek God's will in the middle of a consult; God prompted me to ask the seller if we could pray together. The seller agreed but confided he had not prayed for a very long time. As I prayed, I could sense he was weeping. I felt peace–that God would somehow take care of this seller and I decided to try this impossible listing. I usually didn't share details about my work with my mother, but afterward I called her to ask her to pray for us.

God reminded me that a friend was part of the landowner's organization. We wrote a letter to the president to plead my client's case. Because of the organization's high list price for the land, the unit's estimated sale price was around $225,000 to $245,000. I attached net estimates and current comps to show that my seller would have to bring upwards of $45,000 cash to close. We begged the organization for mercy and to reduce their land price.

The organization did not lower the land price; after all, they were running a business. But God used the letter for another purpose. My friend who had connected us invited me and my client to sit at his table at the annual Hawaii Prayer Breakfast. Amazingly, my client made time in his schedule and heart to attend. I'm sure he felt God's love through the speakers who were there. We were even introduced to the president to whom we had written! I don't know exactly what my client was feeling, but I think it was God's way of working healing in his heart.

I visited my parents in New York for the Christmas holidays. My mother had continued to pray for my client's faith, and asked how the listing was going. I told her we had sat on the market for four months and asked her to keep praying for my seller.

A couple of days later, on Christmas Eve, we got an offer. We had listed for $295,000, which was very aggressive but would give my sellers a small amount in proceeds. The offer was for $250,000–above my estimates–but it still meant the sellers would have to bring cash to close. My seller wanted to reject it outright. Since it was right on the holiday, I asked him to take a couple of days to pray on it.

After Christmas, my seller told me he would like to try countering. I explained the seller's situation to the buyer's agent, who is a top agent and–I believe–also a Christian. We were able to come to an amazing agreement: over-market value at $265,000–at that price, my seller would just break even! The ensuing escrow was full of tough negotiations for repairs and closing credits. The buyer's agent pitched in to help, and my seller had to come up with $8,600 cash to close–but it was a doable amount that would allow him to move on from the property and start a new chapter.

After closing, the seller confided that the Christmas timing showed him God had brought this buyer. God's fingerprints were all over this "impossible" sale! I was humbled, because none of us would have been glorifying God had I cancelled the first consult. It was a huge faith-building milestone for me.

I pray we will all have transactions with such an incredible God Layer to them, and that we can be obedient to partner with God and His impossible-busting plans.

Reflect: *Can I find the faith I need to let God reign over my client's "impossible" situation? What can I do to get out of His way?*

Job 42:1-5 (NIV)

"Then Job replied to the Lord:

'I know that you can do all things; no purpose of yours can be thwarted.
You asked, 'Who is this that obscures my plans without knowledge?'
Surely I spoke of things I did not understand, things too wonderful for me to know.

'You said, 'Listen now, and I will speak; I will question you, and you shall answer me.'
My ears had heard of you but now my eyes have seen you.'"

Prayer prompt: *Dear Lord, you are almighty God; nothing is impossible for you! As Job said in praise to you, I should not "obscure your plans." Please give me your understanding and wisdom in my situation with __________. Please help me to trust in your power so that I can fully lean on you. I praise you for your unceasing work for me, my clients, and our transaction. In Jesus' name, Amen.*

When your client is grieving

Praying for and with clients

As agents, we walk alongside our clients through milestones such as marriage, divorce, new babies, and empty nests. Illness and death are also times of change for families, and we have some listings because the homeowner has passed away or can no longer live independently. These sellers—and their families—deserve our utmost empathy and sensitivity.

Proverbs 3:27 (NLT)

"Do not withhold good from those who deserve it
when it's in your power to help them."

When the homeowner who has passed away is someone we knew, we join the family in their mourning. But many times, we never knew the homeowner and find ourselves working with grieving family members. We must understand that they are probably overwhelmed as they must grieve while also handling all the affairs that come after a death.

Reflect: ***If I put myself in my client's shoes, how would I be feeling? How can I show them God's love?***

Romans 12:15 (NIV)

"Rejoice with those who rejoice; mourn with those who mourn."

I served a seller who was the trustee of his brother's estate. We never met because he lived on the east coast and his brother's estate was here on Oahu. The brother had recently passed away after an illness, leaving behind three teenage sons. My client was not only grieving the loss of his brother, he was now a father-figure to his three nephews. My client felt a tremendous responsibility to maximize the proceeds from the home sale to fund his nephews' futures.

The boys were still living in the home when I took on the listing. The eldest son was my main local contact. He was kind, responsible, and doing the best he could to guide his younger brothers despite his own need to grieve his father's passing. I found myself trying but failing to build any meaningful rapport with the boys. I suppose they had good reason to feel uncooperative toward me; I was the person they perceived to be kicking them out of the home that held precious memories of their father. I tried to offer up condolences and encouragement, but my attempts always felt inadequate and hollow.

When we are helping other sellers who have a great reason to sell–such as a job promotion or baby on the way–it's not difficult for them to find the motivation and energy to get the home ready for sale. But for family members who are grieving, the added responsibility of selling a home can be totally overwhelming. Funds to do even the minimum repairs needed to properly present the listing may be limited. They might be reluctant clearing out the home because there are so many reminders of their loved one.

If we stop and think—better yet, pray and ask God for help—we can empathize better with what our clients are going through. This is when we go the extra mile and show up at 6:00am to help at a garage sale. This is when we exercise patience and don't push our agenda or timeline for the listing. We must be extra faithful with these clients. Let's not become weary of continuously loving them, even if they are unresponsive. Let's be faithful and pray for our clients and their grief.

It's God's way to use everything for His good. After my mother passed away suddenly in early 2020, an unexpected bittersweet blessing was that I suddenly had a deeper empathy for my clients who had also lost a beloved parent. There is a solidarity that can only be experienced when both people have suffered similar pain and loss. When I tell a new client, "I have also lost my mother," I feel their demeanor and heart soften. Sharing something personal with our client can open up deeper communication and rapport.

We may feel compelled to tell our clients we will be praying for them. If we say it with love and sincerity–and actually do what we promise–our gesture should encourage them. God may even give us an opportunity to pray with our client. Although I was very uncomfortable to ask at first, over the years I've developed this approach: "I don't know what your faith or beliefs are, but I'm a Christian and I would love to pray for you. Would it be OK if I say a quick prayer right now?" I'm happy to tell you that God has given a 100% success rate of my clients answering yes; He will provide the same for you!

Romans 12:9 (NIV)

"Love must be sincere."

Reflect: *How can I find more empathy to help my clients who are in fragile emotional states?*

Prayer prompt: *Jesus, you are my inspiration and source of knowing how to love people. I am helping my client __________ through a difficult time of loss. Please give me more understanding of what they're going through. Please help me show your love, even when they're not responsive. In your name, Amen.*

When you might advise a seller not to sell

Do the right thing

During my first few years in the business, all of my sellers' situations had positive outcomes; they all walked away with a nice proceeds check. The first time a seller had to bring cash to the closing table was a huge shock (and lesson) for me. I had failed in one of my first responsibilities as a listing agent: to calculate the seller's net proceeds by estimating a sale price for the home, then subtracting the various selling costs and mortgage payoff.

Looking back to when those sellers first contacted me, I had been so eager to get a listing lead that I didn't ask what they still owed on the home, nor their reasons for selling. It was a self-centered, rookie move; it was more about me and the potential paycheck, not about looking out for their best interests.

When a seller is close to breaking even–or if they'll need to bring cash to closing–we should have a discussion with them to make sure selling is their best option. If I had done so properly with my seller, we might have approached the pricing and negotiations differently even if they had still decided to sell.

> **1 Corinthians 10:24 (NLT)**
>
> "Don't be concerned for your own good but for the good of others."

Reflect: *When have I put my needs and gain ahead of what's best for my clients? Why did I do that?*

Prayer prompt: *Dear Lord, I want to confess to you if ever my professional actions were motivated by making a paycheck or achieving a personal goal; I ask for your forgiveness. Please help me be more aware if I am doing this in the future. Help me to trust in you to provide all the business and income I need. Help me not to see a client as a paycheck. Help me to understand their motivations and goals so I can help them do what's best.*

After asking the very first question ('Why do you want to sell?') of a prospective seller, we must keep their motivation and goals as our North Star to guide us as we discuss their options. We owe it to them to tell the honest truth and keep their best interests at heart.

Some sellers may have done their own calculations and know they are going to be short; but other sellers may not fully understand the various selling costs and commissions they must pay. After presenting my comparative market and net proceeds analyses at a listing consult, I've had many prospective sellers take a step back and say they need to rethink their options. If when I follow up they tell me they've decided not to sell, although it feels like a loss for me personally, I know deep down I did the right thing.

I've also had many sellers still decide to sell, even after I've advised it may be better to wait to build more equity, or for better market timing. They have their reasons and urgency; it's their decision. As long as we have advised them of the possible cash-to-close outcome, we have kept their best interests in mind and done our job. Next, we need to do everything in our power to reduce their selling costs and increase their sales price.

As for any sellers who decide to hold off or rent the property out for another year, perhaps the Lord wants us to have a longer-term relationship with them. Hopefully, we've started to earn their trust and show we are working in their best interest. We can show our care and professionalism via regular communication and market updates to earn their future business. More importantly, we can seek out The God Layer in this relationship!

I hope this next story of my client, Kandi, encourages you. When we first met, I checked and double-checked if she truly wanted to sell her home. She said yes and proceeded to work very hard to prepare the listing. We had amazing photos taken and lots of showings with positive feedback.

It wasn't until we got a fair offer that Kandi realized she was still too attached to her home. It was the most peaceful sanctuary, surrounded by forest and the sound of a running stream. She requested we reject the offer and cancel the listing, and God gave me the grace to support her decision.

I didn't understand what God was up to then, but I eventually learned how it had been the best decision for Kandi. Over the next several years, she fell ill but was able to live out her final chapters comfortably in her beloved home. I saw how important that home was for her–a restful place to prepare her for heaven.

> **Matthew 6:33 (AMP)**
>
> "But first and most importantly seek (aim at, strive after) His kingdom and His righteousness [His way of doing and being right—the attitude and character of God], and all these things will be given to you also."

This is one of my cornerstone verses for my real estate career and life. In one simple sentence, it holds the key to success on this earth–and for eternity. When we advise our sellers truthfully, we are living this verse. There is no need to fear if we do the right thing; there's no 'losing' a client or sale. God will provide!

A few years later, I helped Kandi's family member Lehua to successfully sell their home. I know that God brought Kandi and Lehua into my life and designed the years-long home sale journey to bring us closer to each other and to Him. Lehua and I still get together and chuckle as we remember how we didn't sell the home the first time. There is no real estate transaction more valuable than the gift of a friendship that honors God.

Prayer prompt: *Dear Lord, please help me to always think first about my sellers' best interests. You have a perfect plan and schedule for their home sale. Please help me to advise my clients honestly and wait for your perfect, God Layer timing. I look forward to cultivating a relationship with them in the meantime!*

When you need to repent

How to find peace

Today you turned to this particular chapter because the title resonated with you, and the Holy Spirit is tugging at your heart. Maybe you snapped at an agent or loan officer? Did you treat a vendor with condescension or disrespect? Are you guilty of putting your own agenda ahead of your client's? Whatever the reason you need to come clean before God, I pray that reading this chapter today will help you confess and feel at peace.

Revelation 3:19-20 (NLT)

"I correct and discipline everyone I love. So be diligent and turn from your indifference.

'Look! I stand at the door and knock. If you hear my voice and open the door, I will come in, and we will share a meal together as friends."

Prayer prompt: ***Thank you, Lord, for leading me to this chapter today. By the end of today's time with you, I want to be sharing a meal together!***

The story of Jonah and the big fish seems so simple–like a fable. From the deck of the ship to the belly of the fish, Jonah knew deep in his heart the cause of God's punishment: he did not obey God and go to Nineveh.

Reflect: ***Read Jonah chapter 1. Jonah disobeyed God's command. What have I done that has pained God? What do I need to repent from?***

There is a direct cause and effect: God told Jonah to go to Nineveh, but "Jonah ran away from the Lord" (NIV) and disobeyed Him. So the Lord sent the storm and Jonah was thrown overboard.

Before he was thrown overboard, Jonah confessed to his shipmates that God was angry with him–it was his sin that caused the whole ship's demise. His heart must have been pierced with guilt to know and admit this. His confession impressed his shipmates (who were non-believers) so much that they prayed and made a sacrifice to God.

Reflect: ***Has my sin caused others hurt or distress? Can I be honest like Jonah and admit my sin? Next, read Jonah chapter 2.***

God provided the fish to come along just at the right time and place. Inside the belly of the fish is where Jonah owns up to God. He clearly recognizes God "hurled [him] into the depths" (NIV), but in the next breath, he is full of praise and confidence that the same God will deliver him. Here is another cause and effect: Jonah's prayers and repentance caused God to save him, and the whale spat him up onto dry land.

God is saddened, even angered, by our disobedience; but just as quickly, He shows mercy as soon as we repent. We often skip the confession part and appeal only to God's forgiving side. But we can't forget the role we played in causing our own troubles. Are we aware we have hurt God with our actions, and do we feel guilty?

Prayer prompt: ***Lord, I am in the belly of the fish. You know all about it–the fish comes from you. It's a rescue plan, but more importantly, it's where I need to repent and praise you for deliverance, like Jonah. I will now repeat Jonah's words as my own cry to you, Lord:***

Jonah 2:2-10 (NLT)

"He said,

'I cried out to the Lord in my great trouble,
and he answered me.
I called to you from the land of the dead,
and Lord, you heard me!
You threw me into the ocean depths,
and I sank down to the heart of the sea.
The mighty waters engulfed me;
I was buried beneath your wild and stormy waves.
Then I said, 'O Lord, you have driven me from your presence.
Yet I will look once more toward your holy Temple.'

'I sank beneath the waves,
and the waters closed over me.
Seaweed wrapped itself around my head.
I sank down to the very roots of the mountains.
I was imprisoned in the earth,
whose gates lock shut forever.
But you, O Lord my God,
snatched me from the jaws of death!
As my life was slipping away,
I remembered the Lord.

And my earnest prayer went out to you
in your holy Temple.

Those who worship false gods
turn their backs on all God's mercies.
But I will offer sacrifices to you with songs of praise,
and I will fulfill all my vows.
For my salvation comes from the Lord alone.'

Then the Lord ordered the fish to spit Jonah out onto the beach."

Reflect: *Take a few minutes to pour out your heart and confession fully to God.*

> **1 John 1:9 (AMP)**
>
> "If we [freely] admit that we have sinned and confess our sins, He is faithful and just [true to His own nature and promises], and will forgive our sins and cleanse us continually from all unrighteousness [our wrongdoing, everything not in conformity with His will and purpose]."

Prayer prompt: *Lord, thank you for hearing my prayers as you heard Jonah's. Thank you for your forgiveness! Now that you have rescued and released me from the fish, I feel __________ and ___________. In your name I praise and thank you God!*

Estranged or broken relationships

Cultivating a heart to reconcile

Estranged or broken relationships happen in life, both inside and outside real estate. When it's with a client, our business and reputation can suffer. Reconciliation with an estranged friend or client is beneficial for not just our business, but also for our heart and soul. Even when we don't feel we were in the wrong, we can still be the one to initiate reconciliation.

I held a very long and stubborn grudge against a close friend from college—for over 10 years. The reason wasn't anything she had said or done to me; I took offense to something she said to a mutual friend. I cut her off and kept my heart hardened, even long after our mutual friend had forgiven her. Besides the dark spot on my heart and conscience, our mutual friends also suffered because of my actions: they could no longer enjoy our group trips and had to tiptoe awkwardly around our rift.

Anytime I heard a sermon about forgiveness or broken relationships, I would think about this friend. For those 10 long years, I knew deep in my heart God was displeased with me. I was a total hypocrite to withhold forgiveness from my friend while preaching to others about forgiveness. I could not complete this book without first reconciling this friendship (and I have!). Who knows what blessings I missed during those years I stubbornly withheld forgiveness?

Ephesians 4:32 (NLT)

"[B]e kind to each other, tenderhearted, forgiving one another, just as God through Christ has forgiven you."

Reflect: *Who do I need to reconcile with? What feelings linger about what happened with this relationship? What can I do on my side of things?*

Prayer prompt: *Dear Lord, I confess that I still feel ___________ about ___________. I ask you to help me replace any blame or negative feelings with your love, kindness, and forgiveness. Please heal me as well as the relationship. In your name, Amen.*

I have another personal story about an estranged client relationship. Early in my career, my pastor referred me to help a family who had moved to the island. We eventually found the perfect home on one of the streets the husband had specifically requested–he was a delivery driver and had scoped out his favorite neighborhoods!

A few years later when they decided to move back to the mainland, the family asked for my help to list the home. Unfortunately, we were not able to sell it during my three-month watch and they withdrew the listing. A few months later and to my surprise, the home was back on the market with another listing agent. I'm ashamed to say I became bitter and let my seller's 'betrayal' stand in the way of our friendship. I cut ties with them–first out of respect for their listing agreement with their new agent. But even after they successfully sold the home, I never reached out.

Many years have passed, but writing this chapter convicted me to finally reach out to the family. I've emailed them and asked for their forgiveness. I remain hopeful they will respond, and that we can reconcile someday. Just as we sometimes can't see The God Layer in the moment, God will reveal His plan in His perfect timing.

As we lift up our broken relationships to God, He will begin to soften all the hearts involved. We can ask Him to direct us what to do next; we can be ready for His right timing and opportunity to reconcile. Even if God doesn't prompt us to act yet, or if the other person isn't open right now, God will give us peace as we wait for His timing. We can continue to pray for a genuine reconciliation.

Once the relationship with our friend or client is mended, we may hear their side of the story. Whatever we hear–or do not hear (as in no apology), I pray God will give us the power to forgive and forget, just as He has forgiven us and forgotten all the many things we've done to hurt Him. Let's let bygones be bygones and focus on joy and gratitude for the renewed relationship!

Colossians 3:15 (NIV)

"Let the peace of Christ rule in your hearts, since as members of one body you were called to peace. And be thankful."

Prayer prompt: *Thank you for guiding me towards reconciliation with __________. Please prepare us both to be ready when your timing comes for us to reconcile. I lift up the relationship to you, Lord!*

When your client chooses another agent

God always has a good reason

I follow some real estate-related social media accounts full of memes about a common and usually painful thing that happens in our business: someone we thought was a friend or had talked with about real estate; a buyer we've taken to see listings; or a seller we've had a consultation with–chooses to work with another agent. Whether or not they were our client to lose, it feels like a loss.

There are also situations where, after working hard for clients, they blame us for not getting their offers accepted or their listing sold. When they switch to another agent, we feel shocked or betrayed. We may second guess if we could have done something better or differently. We may try to cover up our true feelings with ambivalence. We may even feel relieved at not having to work with this person anymore, but our egos are still bruised that we 'lost' them to another agent.

Reflect: ***What are my thoughts and feelings learning __________ has chosen to work with another agent?***

We can be quick to give thanks and praise when the Lord blesses us with a new client. But when He takes a client away, our reaction is usually the opposite. There was one man in the Bible named Job who praised the Lord even when every possible thing and person was taken away from him.

Job 1:21-22 (NIV)

"'Naked I came from my mother's womb,
and naked I will depart
The Lord gave and the Lord has taken away;
may the name of the Lord be praised.'
In all this, Job did not sin by charging God with wrongdoing."

God gives us some clients and not others; He sometimes takes our established clients away. There is always more to the story than we can see. Perhaps our friend didn't choose us in the first place because they don't like to mix friendship and business. Perhaps we need to learn a lesson from failing to communicate or serve a client's needs. Perhaps God is trying to save us from some future pain with a client. Whatever God's reason, even if He doesn't immediately reveal it to us, He is working for us. Like Job, we must trust that God is in control, and that He still loves and cares for us.

Prayer prompt: *Lord, I read here in Job that you give and you also take away. I confess that I feel __________ and __________after finding out that __________ is working with another agent. Please forgive me and calm my bruised ego. Help me to be faithful like Job even when I don't understand why this happened.*

Although we may feel our time and efforts for this client went unappreciated or were for naught, let's banish any thought they were a waste. Even if we weren't hired after the listing consult, didn't we hone our analytical and presentation skills? If we showed properties or marketed the listing, didn't we still gain valuable and transferable market knowledge?

Reflect: *Make a list of good things and knowledge you've gained from your interaction with this client.*

Sometimes if we take the high ground and handle the situation professionally and with grace, the friendship or client may not be totally lost. I've had clients remember how I was gracious in defeat, and either came back around to work with me, or referred me to others! Let's entrust our 'lost' client to the Lord.

> **Romans 8:28 (NIV)**
>
> "And we know that in all things God works for the good of those who love him, who have been called according to his purpose."

Prayer prompt: *Lord, thank you for the time I spent with this client. There are still good things to come out of the experience. Thank you for helping me to see your bigger picture. I know you want the best for me—even when you give me something difficult that tests my faith. I ask that you will bless ___________'s journey with their new agent.*

Should you fire a client?

How to know when to walk away

In our eagerness to serve our clients, we may lose sight of what constitutes a healthy client relationship. We may ignore or justify abuse because we need the paycheck. If you were drawn to this chapter today, you might be questioning whether a client is worth your time, energy, or sanity. It's a serious thing to break ties with a client, so let's lift up our situation to the Lord and ask Him for help.

Reflect: ***Make a list of positives and negatives about working with this client. Why do you think God brought you this client?***

Philippians 4:6-7 (NIV)

"Do not be anxious about anything, but in every situation, by prayer and petition, with thanksgiving, present your requests to God. And the peace of God, which transcends all understanding, will guard your hearts and your minds in Christ Jesus."

Prayer prompt: ***Father God, I come to you today so you can take away my anxiety about my client __________. I ask for more of your wisdom and discernment as I consider my relationship with them. Help me to know if you want me to continue to serve them.***

First, let's consider four possible scenarios that are challenging, but *may not* be sufficient reason for us to quit a client:

- This client is not a good fit for me - God may intentionally connect us to a client whose personality differs from ours. Although these awkward relationships test our patience and communication skills, God wants us to learn how to love all kinds of people.
- This client occasionally acts out due to the normal frustrations of buying or selling a home - Well, this is maybe every client at some point! There are bumps along the way in most transactions; everyone has bad days, including us agents. Hopefully the client apologizes after an outburst; if not, that could be a red flag.
- This client never says 'please' or 'thank you' - Instead of feeling hurt that our client doesn't acknowledge our hard work, we must look to the Lord for our worth and validation.
- This client relationship isn't going anywhere - Although the client's budget or stipulations may make a successful sale seem impossible, we must use compassion and patience. God may have a long-term purpose for having us walk through a longer season together. As we write offers or work hard to sell the listing, God is still using us, and we are still growing as agents.

Reading God's Word always helps us see better, from His perspective. Here are a few verses that might help:

Colossians 3:14 (NLT)

"Above all, clothe yourselves with love, which binds us all together in perfect harmony."

1 Thessalonians 5:14 (NIV)

"And we urge you, brothers and sisters ... encourage the disheartened, help the weak, be patient with everyone."

Romans 15:5 (NLT)

"May God, who gives this patience and encouragement, help you live in complete harmony with each other, as is fitting for followers of Christ Jesus."

Luke 17:9 (TPT)

"Does the servant expect to be thanked for doing what is required of him?"

Reflect: ***Is my situation similar to any of the scenarios above? Which of the Bible verses encourage me? Has my perspective about working with this client changed?***

If your client's behavior goes beyond the scenarios above, review this next list. If any of these serious offenses apply, please consult your broker—and your Broker God—for further help:

- Verbal attacks, which may include frequent profanity or unreasonably harsh criticism.
- A demeaning, condescending attitude.
- Frequent tardiness – not just 10-15 minutes, but 30+ minutes late to appointments without apology or remorse.
- Discriminatory remarks or behavior.

You may feel conflicted: you're reluctant to lose a potential paycheck; you're confused about why the Lord connected you with this client; you're loathe or afraid to endure their bad behavior again. Examine your heart and motives as you question the healthiness of this relationship.

Reflect: ***Do I have confirmation that my client's behavior is harmful? Is there anything else I can do to try to improve or salvage the relationship?***

> **Titus 3:10 (NIV)**
>
> "Warn a divisive person once, and then warn them a second time. After that, have nothing to do with them."

This verse's recommendation to completely cut off a client may seem harsh, but God has our backs! If God gives you confirmation and peace, He will also give you the courage, right words, and opportunity to talk with your client. Envelop the meeting with prayer before, during, and after. If meeting with your client seems daunting to you, ask your broker or another agent to come along as a witness, or ask them to handle the conversation without you. You do not have to face this alone!

Prayer prompt: ***Dear Lord, you know everything that has happened with this client, __________. Lord, what would be the most loving way to move forward? God, if I am still anxious, please give me your peace that passes all understanding. I give all my worries over to you!***

Cultivating your client database

Mining for gold

Some of the first terms we learn in the business are: 'SOI' (sphere of influence), 'contacts,' and 'clients' (as in, we want to turn our contacts into clients). We create a database listing all the people we know or come into regular contact with–classmates, past co-workers, extended family, friends–and their friends. Every time we meet someone new, we are taught to add them to our database.

"Your sphere is a goldmine," says our broker, wanting us to mine our database for potential business. Customer Relationship Management (CRM) systems allow us to add tags or categories. We can mark someone as an active, inactive, or past client. We can rank them according to urgency or priority.

My first broker taught me to focus on those who are 'ready, willing, and able.' Consequently, I may not have spent as much time with buyers who weren't quite ready, or didn't qualify for a mortgage. But do we believe God only wants us to talk with those who can currently afford to own real estate?! Sadly, that leaves so many people out.

In the grand scheme of eternity, isn't showing God's love more important than gaining a new real estate client? This is the real gold we should be mining! We don't want to miss or overlook someone whom God has brought into our life for His reasons.

What if we shift our thinking: instead of categorizing each person as a real estate 'prospect' or 'lead,' shall we see them as our 'neighbor' whom

God commands us to love? No matter whom God puts in front of us, we can be sure He has a God Layer reason!

Matthew 22:36-40 (NIV)

"'Teacher, which is the greatest commandment in the Law?' Jesus replied: "'Love the Lord your God with all your heart and with all your soul and with all your mind.' This is the first and greatest commandment. And the second is like it: 'Love your neighbor as yourself.' All the Law and the Prophets hang on these two commandments.'"

Reflect: *Ask God to bring to mind a few people in your sphere. Why do you think God put them in your life? How might God use you and your relationship for His purpose and glory?*

Prayer prompt: *God, please help me shift how I see the people you've placed in my path. Help me see them with your higher purpose in mind. Thank you for putting each person in my life. Please help me to know your mission and my role for each one.*

Have you ever had a dream about a friend you haven't connected with in ages? Or has someone come to mind out of the blue? God nudges us all the time: are we listening and acting on these important prompts? Action can start with a quick prayer: 'Why this person, and now, God?' Then let Him guide your next steps–perhaps a call, text, or visit.

Another way to seek God's prompting is to regularly review and pray over your database. As you scan the names, ask God to highlight the people He wants you to get in touch with. Let's put aside any ulterior motives related to real estate and instead be led by God's purpose to love them.

I helped a wonderful couple sell their home as they moved into a senior living community. We had a tough time finding a buyer, and the husband asked me to pray a couple times during the listing and transaction. Other than that, I never had a chance to talk about faith with them. A year after our sale closed, the husband went to heaven (his wife's words). Although there is no prospect of any more real estate business with the wife, I feel God calling me to continue the relationship, and we continue to meet regularly for lunch. I'm praying for the God Layer in that friendship to eventually bear fruit.

We get to know our clients on a very deep level as we help them with their transactions. We celebrate and mourn with them through major milestones in their lives. God will not stop using these deep connections just because a transaction has closed–that would be a waste!

Reflect: ***Who is God nudging me about today? What action will I take based on God's prompting?***

Matthew 5:14-16 (NIV)

"You are the light of the world. A town built on a hill cannot be hidden. Neither do people light a lamp and put it under a bowl. Instead they put it on its stand, and it gives light to everyone in the house. In the same way, let your light shine before others, that they may see your good deeds and glorify your Father in heaven."

Let's continue to follow God's promptings to meet with our clients–past and present. Let's look for the people who are treasures even greater than gold in His heart.

Prayer prompt: ***Dear God, thank you for using me as your light to the people around me! I'm never going to be a perfect example, but as I communicate with my sphere, help me to know what to say to encourage and love them-maybe not just in matters of their earthly home, but to ensure they have an eternal home. In Jesus' name, Amen.***

Having faith conversations

Take every opportunity

The 2008 Japanese movie, *Departures*, follows two funeral home workers as they perform services for the families and friends of the deceased. Regret is the key emotion in scene after scene of anguished mourning. The movie's message of *carpe diem* is universal: seize the day and cherish time with loved ones now so you don't have any regrets after they're gone.

Death can happen at any moment. When we hear that a friend or client has passed away, the best-case scenario is if we know for certain they were a believer and can take comfort we will see them in heaven. The worst-case scenario is that we don't know their faith status. My prayer is that we don't miss any opportunities to have faith status conversations.

Reflect: ***How does it feel to lose someone but know they are in heaven with God? How does it feel to lose someone but not know their faith status?***

Isaiah 52:7 (NLT)

"How beautiful on the mountains
are the feet of the messenger who brings good news, the good news of peace and salvation,
the news that the God of Israel reigns!"

The day I started writing this chapter, I attended the 'Celebration of Life' service for my very first client, Ann. I first met her at Maui Divers Jewelry, where her official title was Executive Assistant to the CEO, and her unofficial title—as far as I and many other employees were concerned—was "mother hen." Whenever we needed advice or a shoulder to cry on, Ann's door, ears, and heart were open.

It took a supportive and mother-like friend like Ann to put her trust in me as an untested and brand-new agent. She and her husband hired me to sell an investment property, and I'm sure I forgot or did a million things wrong in that first transaction. But because she had such positive trust in me, my career got off to a great start.

Ann had a long period of illness before she passed away. During that time, we had a conversation about her background, and I discovered her faith status: she had attended a Christian church as a young girl, and with Jesus as her Savior, Ann was not afraid to die. In her last months in hospice at home, God gave me and many other friends opportunities to text her Bible verses, worship songs, and prayers. In Ann's case, I was lucky to have the chance to talk with her about God and have full peace at her passing that she is in heaven.

Reflect: ***When was the last time I shared my faith with someone? What led up to that conversation? Do I actively look for opportunities to share my faith?***

You may feel there is a line drawn where we can't mix business with faith talk—I understand. I once had a manager directly instruct me not to talk about my faith in my monthly client newsletter. (Forgive me, Lord, for not obeying her!) If our hearts are willing and we have the right intent, God will help us know when it's best to hold our tongues or when He is opening an opportunity for a deeper conversation. No manager can fault us if the client is the one who opens up the topic!

I like to hint at my faith in conversation by saying things like:

"Something God is teaching me right now is..."

"I heard an encouraging message at church this week..."

"I'm not sure if you are a praying kind of person, but I am! I'm a Christian, and I will be praying for our transaction."

Gradually, as we share tidbits about our faith, God will work in the hearts of good soil which He is preparing. As our relationships grow deeper, we might share our own testimony, or the salvation invitation in John 3:16. It might take time as we grow the relationship, but I pray that when God gives us an opportunity to lead someone to Jesus, we will seize it with courage! This is the ultimate God Layer in any relationship we have.

Even if we don't get an opportunity to speak about Jesus openly with a client, we can still speak kindness and model a life of faith. God may choose another person in their life to lead them in the salvation conversation–He usually surrounds people with a supporting cast of believers so we can each do our part in bringing them closer to Him. We hold much good power within us to encourage our clients. Let's remember that our words can refresh and give life!

Proverbs 16:24 (TPT)

"Nothing is more appealing than speaking beautiful, life-giving words. For they release sweetness to our souls and inner healing to our spirits."

Prayer prompt: *God, I don't want anyone I love to die without having a chance to hear your good news. I want to be someone who takes every opportunity to talk about you with all those around me. Please hone my sensitivity to your prompting and nudge me to speak with love and boldness every time you give me an opportunity.*

When your buyer's offers keep striking out

Keep the faith!

Working with a buyer to submit an offer is the culmination of much time and effort: we show countless homes, analyze comps, craft the offer, explain the contract language, work with the loan officer, and build rapport with the listing agent. So, one of the hardest phone calls we make as agents is to tell a buyer our offer wasn't accepted. Relaying the bad news can be a letdown not only for our buyer, but for us agents.

Reflect: ***How have my buyers reacted when their offer wasn't accepted? How have I reacted?***

After hearing back from the listing agent, I usually like to take some time to process my own thoughts and feelings before I call my buyers. A quick prayer is always helpful—I can ask God to give me the right words and tone as I talk to my clients, and pray for my clients to be ready to receive the message. I can also pray that any personal feelings don't cloud how I deliver the message.

Prayer prompt: ***Lord, fill my heart with kindness and love as I convey the news to my buyer. Give me empathy and sensitivity to their reactions. Help me to know how best to encourage and support them.***

Sometimes we are reluctant to write an offer we feel doesn't have a chance. Let's put aside our laziness and weariness and continue to support our clients' wishes. Let's search for The God Layer in working with this buyer.

> **Philippians 2:3 (NIV)**
>
> "Do nothing out of selfish ambition or vain conceit. Rather, in humility value others above yourselves"

Most buyers will have a learning curve and our job is to meet them—with patience—wherever they are on their curve. Our job is to explain the current market and competitive circumstances of the listing. We should be careful not to push a buyer to offer or concede more than they're comfortable. The final decision is theirs, and we need to respect all that went into it—some details of which they may not even share with us.

Early in my career, I had a buyer who wanted to write an offer on an extremely underpriced home that had seen a frenzy of activity. As I drafted our offer, I tried to gauge the level of competition and inquired with the listing agent; they told me they already had multiple offers over asking. Still, my Christian buyers insisted: "God told us to offer $X." The number was quite far below asking. I was a little indignant they hadn't listened to my guidance about the strategically low list price. I made the unforgiveable mistake of doubting their faith, and let my feelings show.

As I wrote the offer—more out of duty than any real hope of getting it accepted—God convicted me of my lack of faith. I confessed to my clients that it was wrong of me to doubt and disrespect what they had heard from the Lord. I asked them to forgive me, and we submitted the offer. It was rejected, and the husband gave me a terrible survey rating. They later ended up working with another agent. It was a humbling, but important, lesson for me.

Reflect: ***How should I communicate with my client if I feel their offer doesn't have a good chance of being accepted?***

On the other hand, if we are totally surprised at an offer being rejected, this becomes a big learning for us agents. We can backtrack: was there anything more we could have done to help our buyers? Did we have blind spots when we reviewed the comps? Did we neglect to ask the listing agent what terms and factors were most important to the seller? Could we have consulted with our broker or peers about what they were seeing in winning offers in the current market?

Let's turn this into a learning opportunity for ourselves as agents as well as for our buyers. We can ask the listing agent for feedback about what our offer lacked when compared to the winning offer; this will help our buyers know how to make a stronger offer in the future. We could also check if the sellers would consider us for back-up position.

Each failed offer is an opportunity to learn and deepen our connection with our buyer. As we meet or talk with them, let's stay in tune with their feelings. They will be looking to us for continued encouragement; let's keep the faith on their behalf! Let's convey our hope that God has a beautiful plan for them. If you feel led, perhaps this is a chance to pray with your client or share an encouraging verse.

> **Jeremiah 29:11 (NIV)**
>
> "'For I know the plans I have for you,' declares the Lord, 'plans to prosper you and not to harm you, plans to give you hope and a future.'"

Isaiah 26:3-4 (MSG)

"People with their minds set on you,
  you keep completely whole,
Steady on their feet,
  because they keep at it and don't quit.
Depend on God and keep at it
  because in the Lord God you have a sure thing."

Reflect: *Is there an opportunity here to offer to pray with my client, or share an encouraging Bible verse with them?*

Prayer prompt: *Lord, you are watching over my buyer __________'s journey. My client is feeling __________, and I am feeling __________. I trust that you are working in their lives and that you have the right home waiting for them. Help me to be an encouraging witness so that my faith and confidence in your plan will overflow to also give them hope. In your name I pray, Amen.*

When your buyer's offer is accepted!

Being true fiduciaries

Congratulations—your buyer's offer was just accepted! Say a prayer of thanks to the Lord, have an extra cup of coffee or scoop of ice cream, then fasten your seat belt for the upcoming ride! Now comes the important work of helping our buyer with their due diligence. If there was ever a time to show our buyer love, it is during escrow, when we can truly look out for their best interests.

> **1 John 3:18 (NIV)**
>
> "Dear children, let us not love with words or speech but with actions and in truth."

Reflect: *What does it mean to represent my buyer's best interests? Is there anything that could prevent me from being 100% on their side?*

Nothing should come before our client's best interests—including anticipation for our paycheck. If we equate this new escrow with our own closing day goals, we're inviting trouble. We can't think about closing just yet—let's focus on the escrow hurdles ahead.

Prayer prompt: *Thank you God for this opportunity for my buyers! As we open escrow, guide me to always be on their side as we make 100% sure this is the right property for them.*

Our role is to direct and guide, and also to observe and listen to our buyer. Are they confident (perhaps overly)? Are they nervous or overwhelmed? There are so many emotions associated with buying a home—even for experienced buyers and investors. Let's watch and react quickly when they need our help or encouragement. We can never go wrong by asking: "How are you feeling about everything today?" Let's give them lots of opportunities to share or ask questions.

As we lead them in their due diligence, let's keep in mind our buyer's background and experience—or lack thereof. A first-time buyer will lean more on us to help them know the right questions to ask. Home ownership introduces a new vocabulary and concepts which can be overwhelming. Although we probably explained all the contractual contingencies when our buyer first signed the offer, they may not have felt they were pertinent at the time. Now that the escrow and contract are actually in progress, it's a good idea to review our buyer's options at each juncture.

Reflect: ***From what I know about my buyer's experience and temperament, what can I do to ensure they are feeling comfortable as we go through the transaction?***

Many contracts allow for buyer contingencies; out of fear, we agents may not want to remind our buyer of any contractual rights to cancel. But our fiduciary duty is to remind and advise them if cancelling is on their mind or in their best interests. Arranging a meeting or call gives our client the time and space to talk through their thoughts with us. If we are up against a contractual deadline for a decision, we might even see if the sellers can give us an extra day or two.

Our buyer may just need time to think and catch their breath. Let's listen, then listen some more. We can see how how they are coming to their possible decision to cancel: there may be misunderstandings or miscommunications we can correct. There may be opportunities to add perspective or answer questions so they can make a final decision. In the end, if they decide to cancel, we must show them our genuine support.

> **Proverbs 18:13 (NLT)**
>
> "Spouting off before listening to the facts
> is both shameful and foolish."

I hope reading this chapter doesn't sober any celebratory feelings you have as you and your buyer open escrow. You and your buyer have reached a major milestone, praise God! May He guide you and your buyers on this escrow journey. If you are seeking God and His purpose all the way through, He will give you the right words and ways to support your buyer 100%.

> **1 Chronicles 29:17 (NIV)**
>
> "I know, my God, that you test the heart and are pleased with integrity. All these things I have given willingly and with honest intent."

Prayer prompt: *Dear God, thank you again for entrusting me with this buyer. Please help me to field all their questions with patience, and work diligently on their behalf. Whatever happens, help me to earn my buyer's trust that I am supporting them. We lift up the outcome of this escrow to you. In Jesus' name, Amen.*

When your offer is miraculously accepted

God is always at work in the background

There are times and circumstances when we write an offer and feel it has a very low chance of being accepted. Even so, we must always give it our 100% "best as unto the Lord" (Colossians 3:23). When a miraculous acceptance follows, we agents can be quick to take all the credit. Wasn't it a culmination of our human efforts and knowledge that helped our buyers get into contract?

Reflect: ***Have I ever had an offer that, against all odds, was miraculously accepted? How did my buyer get so lucky?***

> **James 1:17 (AMP)**
>
> "Every good thing given and every perfect gift is from above; it comes down from the Father of lights [the Creator and Sustainer of the heavens], in whom there is no variation [no rising or setting] or shadow cast by His turning [for He is perfect and never changes]."

We may want to take all the credit for the acceptance, but we are never the only ones hard at work! I'd like to share one amazing story which taught me all the glory should always go to God.

I was working with a first-time buyer who had worked to save up enough for a 5% down payment. After a long search, we finally found the perfect place for her to spread her wings. The renovated studio was in a quiet neighborhood and the boutique building had a view of the city and ocean. It was late 2021, in the middle of a record-breaking seller's market, making for tough competition among buyers.

As we prepared our offer, the loan officer we'd been working with for over a year told me his bank could not lend for that building without 30% down. I consulted with the listing agent who'd had other sales in the building. He gave me the name of a bank to try, but I didn't have a go-to loan officer there. I scanned their website and somewhat randomly found a name I recognized; Clint was a loan officer I had crossed paths with but never worked with. I gave him a call, and he was able to check and confirm: they could loan on this building with 5% down! Miracle number one!

We quickly packaged up our full-price offer and submitted it; we had no competition! Miracle number two! But as we waited for the seller's response that didn't come, I had a gnawing fear they'd received another offer. Sure enough, the listing agent confirmed they'd received a full price, all-cash offer soon after ours. He was still waiting on his seller's decision, but mentioned the cash offer was a slam dunk.

I knew this buyer from church, and we prayed together on the phone that God's will would be done. We knew our chances were slim, especially with just 5% down versus all cash. Then I got the call from the listing agent: the seller would give us a chance if we would come up $5,000 over asking. This was my client's first ever offer; she had just boarded the emotional roller coaster that is real estate. We continued to pray, and she wanted to sleep on it. She decided to go for it and we felt victorious as we accepted the counter! Miracle number three!

A few days after we opened escrow, I followed up with Clint since I had never worked with him before. He revealed something crazy: he—our randomly selected loan officer—and the seller were longtime friends! When the seller heard my buyer was hoping to buy her first home, she recalled with empathy when she herself had been a young, first-time buyer, also struggling to have her offers accepted. Feeling confident her friend the loan officer could make it happen, and despite the faster and much easier choice of the all-cash offer, she chose us! Miracle number four!!!

> **John 5:17 (AMP)**
>
> "But Jesus answered them, 'My Father has been working until now [He has never ceased working], and I too am working.'"

The God Layer is like an app on our phone that's set to continuously run in the background. Even if we have the 'God Layer app' closed, God is always working on our behalf—for the good (Romans 8:28)!

I was so humbled to hear the other side of the story—humbled because I gave myself too much credit! It was clear that God's hand was on all sides of this transaction, even where we did not have any control: God had led us to the right loan officer and had worked in the seller's heart.

The cherry on top was that our original closing date was the first week of January, but even through the crazy holiday schedule, our loan officer closed early, before the end of the year. This was in the best interests of both the seller and my buyer! Miracle number five!

> **Romans 4:4-5 (MSG)**
>
> "If you're a hard worker and do a good job, you deserve your pay; we don't call your wages a gift. But if you see that the job is too big for you, that it's something only God can do, and you trust him to do it—you could never do it for yourself no matter how hard and long you worked—well, that trusting-him-to-do-it is what gets you set right with God, by God. Sheer gift."

Reflect: *Have I ever had something happen that was so good and miraculous, it could only have been because God was working?*

Prayer prompt: *Dear God, thank you for working hard in the background for our good, even when I am not aware. Forgive me for forgetting to pray; forgive me for forgetting to give you credit! You are almighty, all-powerful, and all-knowing! Please help me remember that you are the ultimate resource and giver of all good things.*

Launching a listing and presenting offers

Meaningful communication with sellers

Launching a listing is the culmination of much preparation and research. There may have been months–or even years–between when you first met the seller and when they and the property are ready. Decluttering and purging, staging and cleaning, research and analysis, phone calls and paperwork–much work has already been done. Now with activation, it's showtime!

The days immediately before and after launching a listing can be a whirlwind of tasks and inquiries. Amid the hustle, let's make time to dedicate this client relationship to God's will and mercy. We never quite know the road coming up ahead–but God does.

Reflect: ***How did I first meet this seller? How are our communication and relationship so far? How have we handled any obstacles or rough patches? Do I have any ideas yet about why God has put them in my life?***

Prayer prompt: ***Thank you, God, for my seller, __________ and our new listing! I am thankful you've helped us on our journey so far–for example, with __________ and __________. As we launch the listing, I ask for your blessing on the property and our relationship.***

Regular and open communication will enrich our connection with our seller, elevating it from a mere business transaction to a meaningful relationship. It takes time and effort to learn the best way to approach each client. Even if our client is a friend or family member we think we know already, this transaction will add new facets to the relationship–perhaps God will reveal The God Layer He has been planning and building up to all this time!

Email is good for documentation and sending attachments; texts are good for quick updates. Some clients may insist these are their preferred ways to reach them, but nothing beats a phone or video call for true connection. True connection is why God has placed us in this job! There are many junctures during a listing where too much could be lost in translation (or abbreviation) over email or text. Sellers crave phone and in-person communication more than they realize. Our relationship and transaction will be all the better for it.

It's easy to call the seller when we need paperwork, or a question answered. But it's also a good practice to call them even without an agenda, just to check in. I usually find out there's something they were wondering about and wanting to ask me. And if not, it's a great opportunity to deepen the relationship and simply chat from a place of caring. We can ask about what's happening with them outside of the transaction and grow our relationship.

Proverbs 18:21 (AMP)

"Death and life are in the power of the tongue,
And those who love it and indulge it will eat its
fruit and bear the consequences of their words."

Prayer prompt: *Jesus, please nudge me when you want me to call a particular client. Give me love and compassion as I listen to them. Help me find the right words at the right time, and to bear the good fruit of meaningful communication with them!*

Things become exponentially more complicated if we have multiple sellers on title or when our sellers are getting divorced. If only one of the sellers calls us, we can follow up afterward with a recap to the other seller(s). I had a particularly challenging listing with five decision makers in five time zones and usually they were not on the same page. I had to work much harder than usual because I had to have many separate conversations and follow-up emails. The goal should be for all our clients to feel they are being heard and receiving the same information at the same time.

If we are caught in a contentious situation, we must be careful not to take sides. It's important to remain neutral so every stakeholder feels supported. We can consult with our broker or mentor for any specific advice. Let's be the arbiters of peace and cooperation with our sellers, even when their conversations with one another might be full of conflict.

Reflect: ***Have I ever found myself in the middle of my clients' personal conflict? How did I handle this? How can I pray for them?***

As offers start to come in, let's take care to present each and every offer without prejudice. Some states and brokerages have banned buyer 'love letters' to prevent unconscious bias. You may consider giving a general caution about the protected classes in fair housing.

We can explain to our sellers that their decision should be based on the strength or weakness of each offer's price and terms. We can do our due diligence with the buyer's agent and loan officer and share all pertinent information with the seller. We should go over the contract's fine print in case there is anything the seller may have glossed over or not understood. Possible risks and buyer contingencies should be mentioned both verbally and in writing.

All this work we do to objectively present offers should give our seller confidence that we are sharing all the information we know and are vested in their full understanding. I pray God will help us communicate with our sellers with care, honesty, and upright motives so they can make the right decisions.

> **2 Corinthians 8:21 (NLT)**
>
> "We are careful to be honorable before the Lord, but we also want everyone else to see that we are honorable."

Prayer prompt: *Dear God, thank you again for connecting me with my seller(s) ___________. You have a purpose for our relationship and will give me opportunities to get to know them through a deeper level of communication. Please direct me as to how and when to speak and act for your glory. However this listing's journey progresses, give us your favor and help me continue to work hard for my seller and for you.*

When your listing isn't selling

Eternal optimism

You and your seller launched the listing optimistic you'd have a great response. You were hopeful of getting into contract quickly, maybe even against current market odds. Unfortunately, time has passed without an acceptable offer.

Reflect: ***How am I feeling about this listing? Do I know how my sellers are feeling?***

Most sellers want to have the home sold quickly so they can move on to the next chapter. It's our job to get them the highest possible price while saving them as much in selling and holding costs as possible. Time is money and we are on the clock—even with sellers who insist they aren't in a hurry to sell!

Our seller may outwardly appear cool as a cucumber, but they could be the type to hide or bury their emotions or stress. It's good for us to check in with them regularly; let's lovingly give them opportunities to share how they are doing. Often, after a month or two on the market, they may finally tell us about circumstances they've never mentioned before, perhaps because they assumed we would get into contract more quickly. As we receive new information, we should make any adjustments as needed to work for the seller's best interests and timing.

Romans 12:12 (NIV)

"Be joyful in hope, patient in affliction, faithful in prayer."

Sometimes it can be hard to report to our sellers when we're not getting many showings or offers. While we want to be positive and hopeful, let's report honestly when we didn't have any showings, or receive negative feedback from buyers and agents. If we are passing everything—good and bad—along to our sellers, we'll all be on the same page if we start to see a pattern in the feedback. It will be easier to reach a consensus on changes that may be needed.

The phrase "eternal optimist" refers to someone with unlimited positivity—even when things aren't going well. It doesn't mean ignoring the facts. We owe it to our seller to be pragmatic and point out when we are in a tough situation. We must work harder and communicate more deeply with our sellers when their listings lie dormant. I don't think the phrase "eternal optimist" has any religious origin, but we can adopt that connotation with The God Layer in mind! Let's be tireless in our efforts, guidance, and prayers!

Reflect: *How can I guide my seller with hope and optimism?*

Colossians 3:23-24 (NIV)

"Whatever you do, work at it with all your heart, as working for the Lord, not for human masters, since you know that you will receive an inheritance from the Lord as a reward. It is the Lord Christ you are serving."

Prayer prompt: *Thank you, Lord, for giving me this listing assignment. Keep me hopeful in your miracles and help me pass on your eternal optimism to my*

seller. Forgive me if I have had doubts or negative feelings about this listing. Encourage me so I can encourage my seller!

A good way to gauge our listing's activity is by continuing to monitor and present our sellers with the comps' and general market activity. Sometimes our listing's slow start and days on market are in line with others currently on the market. We should not use this as an excuse, but it is a good encouragement and reminder for our seller if other sellers are in the same boat. This could launch further discussion, perhaps to ask if they'd like to strategize about how to beat out competing listings.

If our listing is noticeably lagging versus the rest of the market, we can pray about having a heart-to-heart talk with our seller. Although we might have known all along our listing would face an uphill battle, this is not the time to say, 'I told you so.' Maybe now they will listen to our original recommendations about improving the listing's condition or price. This is the time to create common ground and remind them we are on the same team. Our seller will hopefully take heart that we are working toward the same goal, even if the news we are giving them is hard to hear.

There will be cases where it becomes clear it's not the right time for the listing or the seller's circumstances may force a new direction. We need to be ready—with the seller's best financial and personal interests in mind—to review other available options. This should be a two-way conversation, possibly requiring consultation with their certified public accountant, financial planner, and/or property manager, so the seller can make their best, informed decision. We should not be discouraged about any consequences to us from a withdrawn listing. This is not about us; it's about what's best for our client.

2 Chronicles 15:7 (AMP)

"But as for you, be strong and do not lose courage, for there is reward for your work."

I was a cheerleader in high school, and our squad had a range of cheers: some were to be used when our team was winning, others when we were losing. We are the cheerleaders for our clients! As believers, if we are to be eternal optimists for them, we can look to the Lord as our source of hope and guidance. Our clients' moods often follow our lead, so let's lead with positivity and hope. Faith and prayer are inherently optimistic.

Reflect: *Might God create an opportunity with my seller's current situation to initiate praying with them?*

Prayer prompt: *Dear God, please help me with this listing for my seller ___________. Help us to have honest and open communication as we discuss what we can do for our listing. If it's your plan, please give me the right opportunity and words to pray with my seller. Help my faith and hope in you so I can be a light for my seller. In Jesus' name, Amen.*

When your seller cancels the listing

With the grace of God

Cancelling a listing is usually a downer—both for our seller and for us. There may be a variety of reasons the listing didn't sell: the market timing wasn't right; buyers didn't accept the home's condition or price; or the seller didn't accept any of the offers presented. If it's been a difficult listing, or your relationship with the seller wasn't copacetic, you might be relieved. You might also worry you've lost the client and a paycheck.

On the other hand, if you helped the seller re-evaluate their goals and the current market, you may both feel at peace that the cancellation is in their best interests. You should feel assured you were able to help your seller make the right decision, and you can keep in contact with them.

Reflect: ***How am I feeling about the cancelled listing? What am I proud of doing for this seller and listing? Do I have any regrets?***

Regardless of how or why the listing is ending, you've worked extremely hard for months. It's totally normal to have feelings of failure, disappointment, or frustration. However, don't let any negative feelings detract from all the work you've done. Remember: from even before you met this seller and won the listing, God was in control. As the listing cancels, God is still in control! Take a few moments to acknowledge the Lord's perfect plan and thank Him for this opportunity and journey.

Prayer prompt: ***Lord, I feel lots of emotions today: __________ and __________. I know you led me to this seller __________, and you helped and***

guided us through this listing. You knew back at the beginning this would be the outcome—and you are still working out your plan! Thank you for this outcome, even though I may not fully understand your purpose. I lift my seller and the home up to you; please continue to bless them.

Habakkuk 3:17-19 (NLT)

"Even though the fig trees have no blossoms,
and there are no grapes on the vines;
even though the olive crop fails,
and the fields lie empty and barren;
even though the flocks die in the fields,
and the cattle barns are empty,
yet I will rejoice in the LORD!
I will be joyful in the God of my salvation!
The Sovereign LORD is my strength!
He makes me as surefooted as a deer,
able to tread upon the heights."

Ending on a professional and friendly note is always ideal. Keeping the lines of communication open with our seller could lead to opportunities to work together again in the future. If the seller makes it known they don't wish to continue communication, we can acknowledge this graciously. Let's trust God and let the client initiate future contact.

Sellers may or may not tell us their true motivations or reasons for cancelling. We don't necessarily need to know; it may have nothing to do with us. Unfortunately, though, some sellers may not feel able to be fully transparent with us. They may feel uncomfortable delivering bad news or feedback.

I had an ending with a seller where my perception of the relationship and the seller's feelings was completely off. Although we'd received three solid offers, none were fully acceptable to him. As he rejected them, he continuously told me he wasn't in a hurry because he didn't have plans to leave the island for another six months. After two months, we withdrew the listing amicably (I thought), and he told me he'd be in touch closer to the time he would be moving. Within a few weeks, however, I saw he had listed with another agent; he also wrote a negative review about me. It was a shock I didn't see coming. Despite feeling hurt, this happened while I was in the middle of writing this book. God gave me His grace so I could forgive this client and give my hurt feelings over to Him.

If we sense our client wasn't happy with us, we can be brave and ask them for honest feedback. Hearing their constructive criticism will help us improve next time with them or other sellers. Being open to their feedback can also change our seller's perception of us for the better; with a heart-to-heart talk, they might even change their mind and continue with the listing.

John 14:27 (AMP)

"Peace I leave with you; My [perfect] peace I give to you; not as the world gives do I give to you. Do not let your heart be troubled, nor let it be afraid. [Let My perfect peace calm you in every circumstance and give you courage and strength for every challenge.]"

2 Corinthians 4:1 (AMP)

"Therefore, since we have this ministry, just as we received mercy [from God, granting us salvation, opportunities, and blessings], we do not get discouraged nor lose our motivation."

My friend, take some time to rest. Give yourself a short mourning period; you've poured your efforts for this listing. By and with the grace of God, I pray you can trust Him and let go. He already has plans for new blessings!

Prayer prompt: *Thank you, Lord, for teaching me so many things during this listing, like __________ and __________. By and with your grace, help me love __________ as we end this current chapter working together. I know that your true purpose and calling for me is not to close sales, but to have fruitful relationships with my clients. Please guide me with whatever you have planned for any future chapters with __________.*

When your buyer feels uneasy during escrow

Advocacy starts with listening

I have a video of my nephew Noah when he was just seven and on his very first roller coaster ride, Big Thunder Mountain at Disneyworld. As the ride starts, my brother points the camera at Noah, who is sitting next to him. Noah is all smiles and joyful cackles during the first few gentle ups and downs. But after the first major drop and sudden scary turn, Noah's face shows a mixture of nausea and concern, then the video ends abruptly. Off-camera, my brother immediately was there to comfort him.

We have a similar role helping buyers navigate the escrow roller coaster. They've already faced some ups and downs as they searched for the right property, made an offer (or two ... or five), and negotiated back and forth with the seller. Once we are in contract, buyers feel the full gravity of the situation. Their mood can quickly shift from the mountaintop high of the acceptance to the terror of the unexpected drops and turns in transaction. As we sit next to them and try to gauge whether they're enjoying the ride, we can step in at the first signs of panic.

Reflect: ***Does my buyer seem uneasy about something? Have I asked what's bothering them? What is a good game plan for us to discuss further?***

Before we have that conversation with our buyer, we can start praying for them. Even when we don't know how or what to pray for, we have our own Helper—the Holy Spirit.

Romans 8:26 (AMP)

"In the same way the Spirit [comes to us and] helps us in our weakness. We do not know what prayer to offer or how to offer it as we should, but the Spirit Himself [knows our need and at the right time] intercedes on our behalf with sighs and groanings too deep for words."

Prayer prompt: *Holy Spirit, you and God the Father already know exactly how my buyer __________ is feeling. Thank you for being my helper! Knowing this gives me strength and confidence so I can help them. Fill my heart with empathy; open my ears to truly listen; and guide me to ask the right questions.*

John 14:26 (AMP)

"But the Helper (Comforter, Advocate, Intercessor—Counselor, Strengthener, Standby), the Holy Spirit, whom the Father will send in My name [in My place, to represent Me and act on My behalf], He will teach you all things. And He will help you remember everything that I have told you."

We agents can take cues from the Holy Spirit as we also help, comfort, advocate and intercede for, counsel, strengthen, and stand by our client. Counselors must first ask lots of questions—and listen—before they can understand and diagnose a problem. A good starting point is an open question such as, 'How are you feeling about everything?' Pause and give the buyer space to think through their reply.

Our clients may answer with a plethora of emotions: they're feeling overwhelmed, remorseful, nervous, unsure. We can listen, our hearts open, with the goal of truly understanding their feelings. We can confirm what we're hearing, possibly with follow-up questions:

- 'Thank you for sharing that you're feeling overwhelmed. Is it from our transaction, or is there anything else going on in your life?'
- 'Thank you for sharing that you're feeling buyer's remorse. What specifically are you regretting? If you could change something about the transaction to help you feel less remorseful, what would that be?'
- 'Thank you for sharing that you're feeling nervous. Are there any questions I can ask or requests for additional information I can make to help you feel more comfortable?'
- 'Thank you for sharing that you're feeling unsure. Is there anything I can do or explain that might help?'

As we listen, we're allowing our client to peel back the layers to find what's at the core of their unease. The first steps of advocacy are asking questions and listening with empathy. Let's be patient as we draw them out—they themselves may not realize how, why, or what they are feeling! We may not need to say much at all. Sometimes the space to share with us and talk through their feelings is all they need. Once they and we know what's going on with them, we can continue advocating on their behalf and take whatever action is needed.

Buying a property is full of unknowns. Although we've probably prepared our buyer beforehand, they will need refreshers as topics come up during escrow; we should not be impatient or irritated that they are asking again. Also, as new information about the property surfaces through inspections and disclosures, buyers will need our help to analyze and weigh any new findings and possible costs. If something is out of our scope, we can refer them to the right expert: loan officer, attorney, accountant, or tradesperson. Let's help our buyers get whatever information they need to feel confident about their decision to buy. Let's continuously ask, 'Do you have any questions?'

Whatever our buyer asks of us—no matter how minor or impossible it might seem—let's take their request seriously and find the best way to present it to the other side. It is not our place to make any assumptions about how the seller might respond; our position is to relay the request. I've been surprised so many times by a seller agreeing to my buyer's requests.

This time in escrow is our chance to make our buyer feel we have their back 100%. Let's remember we have the Holy Spirit advocating for us as we advocate for our client!

Prayer prompt: *Lord, I am helping my client __________ through their due diligence on this property. I may not know what exactly to pray for, but Holy Spirit, thank you for interceding on our behalf. Help my first and only focus to be my role as my buyer's support and advocate.*

When an escrow cancels

Continued service and love

Escrows are cancelled more often than we agents would like, and for all kinds of reasons. We usually have to process and regulate our own emotions first before ministering to our clients' needs.

Reflect: ***What thoughts and emotions am I processing with this cancelled escrow? Make a list of positive things to come out of this cancellation.***

We may look back and feel our hard work has been a waste of time and energy. We may be discouraged by the delay—or possible ultimate loss—of the commission we were looking forward to. A cancelled escrow can feel like one of the lowest points in our job.

Hopefully you were able to list some good outcomes. Has our client become better informed? Have we learned more about their needs, wants, and personality? Has our relationship with this client deepened? God is still at work!

> **Hebrews 6:10 (NIV)**
>
> "God is not unjust; he will not forget your work and the love you have shown him as you have helped his people and continue to help them."

Prayer prompt: ***Dear God, thank you for knowing my feelings, negative and positive. Help me to see The God Layer at work even through this cancelled***

escrow. This is just one juncture in my long-term relationship with my client; may you use it for good. Thank you for taking care of all my needs.

John 13:12-15 (NLT)

"After washing their feet, he put on his robe again and sat down and asked, 'Do you understand what I was doing? You call me 'Teacher' and 'Lord,' and you are right, because that's what I am. And since I, your Lord and Teacher, have washed your feet, you ought to wash each other's feet. I have given you an example to follow. Do as I have done to you.'"

This passage reminds us that our ultimate calling is to follow Jesus' example as a humble servant. Can we picture ourselves kneeling at our client's stinky feet and lovingly washing and drying them? What kind of attitude would that take?

Even though the cancelled escrow may seem like a dead end right now, we are far from being finished serving and loving our client. Let's continue to follow Jesus' model of service and love. Our client needs us more than ever during this painful juncture.

Prayer prompt: *Lord, please replace my selfish thoughts with care and concern for my client. Help me understand how they may be suffering after this failed escrow. Give me a servant's attitude so I can love them as you would.*

If it's our **buyer** who has cancelled, consider:

Are they feeling discouraged about finding a home? Are they on a deadline to move? Are they considering finding a rental instead? If they are ready for you to send more listings have their search criteria or budget changed?

Scheduling a coffee date or phone/video call to debrief with the client would be an opportunity to answer their questions, listen as they share their feelings, and give encouragement. Prepare for the meeting with prayer and consider in advance some directions in which the conversation might go.

Reflect: ***What have I learned about my buyer? What did they learn about themselves?***

After an escrow and cancellation, I've had weary buyers suggest we take a break. This might make us fearful of losing them as a client, but with a positive and optimistic attitude, we can reassure them we want to honor their wishes. We can ask them if it's OK to still send listings for their consideration. Trust me, they're not going to break the habit of looking at listings online! Usually, they'll get right back in the saddle and reach out to us once something catches their eye. Let's stay in touch and check in regularly; and remember, it doesn't need to be about real estate.

If it's our **seller** who had a cancellation, consider:

Are they already in the process of moving? Are their holding costs mounting? Do they want to withdraw the listing, or go back on the market? Our seller will want to know the buyer's reasons for cancelling; we can try to find out as much as we can from the buyer's agent.

Reflect: ***What have I learned about my seller or the property through this escrow, its inspections, and disclosures? Has the market shifted? Do we need to update anything for the listing?***

If we're motivated by our client's best interests, we will always do the right thing. The time we spend with them will never be wasted; the Lord will honor this time and the relationship. I've had buyers who never bought, as well as sellers who withdrew their listing, still send me referrals. God is always at work and always has our back!

Isaiah 55:8-9 (NIV)

"'For my thoughts are not your thoughts, neither are your ways my ways,' declares the Lord. 'As the heavens are higher than the earth, so are my ways higher than your ways and my thoughts than your thoughts.'"

Prayer prompt: *Thank you for wanting the best for me, and for my client, ___________. I lift them up to you—you have a perfect plan for them. Please bless them and give them comfort. Help me to see The God Layer in my relationship with them, so I can partner with you as we continue our journey. In Jesus' name, Amen.*

When you're frustrated with your client

Loving communication

In our client relationships, there are countless junctures for tension. God created unique personalities and designed human relationships to have times of friction so He can teach us how to love better. So how can we show God's love when we're not getting along with our client?

I initially titled this chapter, "When your client frustrates you." But as I began writing, God revealed it's unfair to blame the client; we agents are at least half the problem! In a friendship or marriage, both parties should compromise and meet in the middle. But in an agent-client relationship, the responsibility for tending to the relationship lies with us agents. We must flex and figure out a better way to meet our clients where they are. Instead of blaming the client, let's repair our attitude.

Reflect: ***I turned to this chapter today with a particular client in mind: __________. Why am I frustrated with our relationship or communication?***

Prayer prompt: ***Dear Jesus, help me have an open heart and mind today as I read your teaching, and change my attitude as I work with __________. I confess any frustration or negativity I've had. Please help me start a fresh chapter.***

Texts and email never convey all that's going on 'between the lines.' A heart-to-heart conversation can be a turning point in a relationship. You or your client may be reluctant to meet, but the simple act of initiating a meeting and showing we want to listen can start to soften the tension. Even if the conversation starts awkwardly, commit to reconciliation. If you bring the Lord along, He will bring you and your client together—don't end the meeting until you can end it positively.

> **James 1:19-20 (AMP)**
>
> "Understand this, my beloved brothers and sisters. Let everyone be quick to hear [be a careful, thoughtful listener], slow to speak [a speaker of carefully chosen words and], slow to anger [patient, reflective, forgiving]; for the [resentful, deep-seated] anger of man does not produce the righteousness of God [that standard of behavior which He requires from us]."

Reflect: ***Which of these three things do I struggle with most with this client: listening carefully, being slow to speak, or being slow to anger?***

As James teaches, loving communication starts with careful and thoughtful listening. We can watch our client's expressions and body language, make eye contact, and not interrupt them. We may be frustrated, but our clients are probably just as frustrated we aren't 'getting' them. If our client is saying the same thing over and over, it might be that they feel we haven't fully heard them.

Next, James teaches us to be slow to speak and slow to anger. Do we show our impatience by responding to our clients too quickly? Does our client sense when we are speaking out of frustration? Are we the fool in the verse below?

> **Proverbs 18:2 (NIV)**
>
> "Fools find no pleasure in understanding but delight in airing their own opinions."

I am guilty of hearing the first part of a client's sentence, assuming the rest, and shutting off listening. Every client and situation are different; how could I know every pain point and background experience *this* client has had? Let's listen to understand where our clients are coming from and what has shaped their thinking.

> **Proverbs 15:1 (NLT)**
>
> "A gentle answer deflects anger,
> but harsh words make tempers flare."

Our clients react to how we talk to and treat them. If we first improve our attitude and pause to listen with humility, our gentle tone and words will be received by our client and we can allow God to heal the relationship.

God placed this client in our path, so we must continue our responsibility to His God Layer to be as Christ-like a witness as we can. We choose what effect our words have: do we want them to wound, or heal?

Prayer prompt: *Please help me find more of your love and gentleness for this client. I want a fresh start with them; help me initiate and foster better communication. Please prepare me to listen to my client with patience, then to think before speaking. Thank you for improving my communication skills, Lord! In your name I pray, Amen.*

When you feel attacked by your client

"The meek will inherit the earth"

There are clients who never seem satisfied with our service or don't communicate any appreciation. Although feeling unappreciated is humbling, silence is preferable to a client who is openly critical. What do we do when a client voices doubt or distrust in us, or blatantly tells us we're wrong? This type of personal attack truly tests us.

Reflect: ***How do I feel when my client is critical of me? Do I tend to clam up, or do I lose my temper? How can I bring my hurt feelings to the Lord?***

Psalm 57:1-3 (NIV)

"Have mercy on me, my God, have mercy on me,
  for in you I take refuge.
I will take refuge in the shadow of your wings
  until the disaster has passed.

I cry out to God Most High,
  to God, who vindicates me.

He sends from heaven and saves me,
  rebuking those who hotly pursue me—
  God sends forth his love and his faithfulness."

Prayer prompt: ***Spend a few minutes crying out to the Lord and ask for His comfort. If you can't find words, open up Psalm 57 and read the whole chapter out loud as your prayer to God.***

I think it's God's all-knowing genius that He included Psalms in the Bible. The psalmist models that it's OK to vent our pain and hurt to the Lord. Let's cry out to God, not our client.

Next, we can ask for His help to pivot our feelings away from anger and towards meekness. Here are three definitions with synonyms for the word "meek" in the Merriam-Webster Dictionary:

1. Enduring injury with patience and without resentment: MILD.
2. Deficient in spirit and courage: SUBMISSIVE.
3. Not violent or strong: MODERATE.

The synonyms match qualities the Bible teaches: mild, submissive, and moderate. Another definition of meekness is 'strength under control.' It's easy to lose our temper; it's much harder to rein it in. When we are under attack, we must control our response.

As for the second definition above, "deficient in spirit and courage," we may be downcast, but we will never be deficient: we can always draw upon God's infinite supply of courage.

Proverbs 29:11 (NLT)

"Fools vent their anger,
but the wise quietly hold it back."

Holding back our temper might cause ulcers, so let everything out to the Lord in prayer. It's difficult to endure a client's criticism and not feel resentment, or to be mild and moderate in our reaction to our client, but God can help us if we ask.

Prayer prompt: ***Lord, help me practice meekness with my client by being mild, submissive, and moderate. I want to listen with humility, be slow to respond, and slow to anger. Fill me with your light and courage!***

As we listen to our client's critique, we can focus on the message and forgive the client's charged emotions or delivery. Also, is there a modicum of truth to their critique? Has there been any misunderstanding? After listening, we may need to calm ourselves, adopt a meek attitude, then thoughtfully respond. If we don't give in to the client's drama and instead defuse the emotion, we can keep the situation from escalating.

All this is easy for me to write and for you to read in a vacuum, yet much harder to put into practice. One habit we can develop is to continuously ask the Lord for help throughout the day, in the moment, throughout every conversation. If we do this, we can ask the Lord for help while under attack.

> **Luke 12:11-12 (TPT)**
>
> "When people publicly accuse you ... do not be troubled. Don't worry about defending yourself or how to answer their accusations. Simply be confident and allow the Spirit of Wisdom access to your heart, and in that very moment he will reveal what you are to say to them."

Prayer prompt: ***Dear Jesus, help me own up to any truths in my client's critique. Help me to forgive their hurtful delivery. I want to have your meekness, your controlled strength. Guard my tongue and give me loving words instead. In your name, Amen.***

When you close a (happy) transaction

Giving thanks

Hallelujah! You just closed a sale!

> **Psalm 84:11 (AMP)**
>
> "For the Lord God is a sun and shield; The Lord bestows grace and favor and honor; No good thing will He withhold from those who walk uprightly."

Reflect: ***Think back over how God first brought you this client. Why do you think God gave you this client and transaction—what was/is The God Layer here? How was God's timing?***

The last question is rhetorical: of course, God's timing is always perfect—sometimes just in the nick of time, but still on time! It is good for us to reflect on how this transaction came at the right time in our lives and career, whether it's because we needed the income, the lessons learned, or this relationship in our lives.

Prayer prompt: ***Lord, I give praise and thanks to you for helping me complete this transaction. You provided this client __________ at the right time—you are Almighty God! I thank you especially for __________. Now, help me to continue to live out your purpose for this relationship.***

Reflect: ***What is God's next assignment for me with this client?***

1 John 4:7 (AMP)

"Beloved, let us [unselfishly] love and seek the best for one another, for love is from God; and everyone who loves [others] is born of God and knows God [through personal experience]."

Do you like to give your clients a closing gift? My go-to closing gift is an invitation for lunch or dinner together. It's an opportunity to celebrate and debrief after the transaction. I am often surprised to learn more about how my client was feeling and thinking throughout the transaction. For example, one client confided her reason for selling was that she and her husband were getting divorced. Once she shared this, many things became clearer in hindsight. I don't think anything would have changed during the transaction had I known sooner, but had I not invited her to lunch, I may never have known. God added a new layer and reason to have compassion for her going forward.

Breaking bread is the surest way to deepen a relationship. We behave differently as we sit at a table and relax. Celebrating our closing is an easy excuse to make the time to get together. It shows our client they mean more to us than just the transaction. The meal can be scaled for our budget—it's not about how extravagant or nice the restaurant is; it's about spending quality time with our client. If your client is not living nearby, a handwritten thank you card is just as meaningful.

If you like to give a material gift, you can keep your ears peeled during the transaction for any hobbies or needs your client shares. Do they like to read? Do they follow a particular sports team? Pray for the Lord to give you an idea for a unique, meaningful gift. The client will feel your love and care as they realize you were paying attention to them.

Beyond any gift, let's mean what we say if we say, 'Let's keep in touch.' God has given us this relationship for His purposes. Even after the transaction is over, let's continue to be good stewards of this gift.

Prayer prompt: *Dear God, what closing gift would you have me give to __________? More importantly, how can I continue the relationship into the future? Please remind me to create opportunities to keep in touch with them. I want to continue your God Layer ministry here! In Jesus' name, Amen.*

When you close a (difficult) transaction

Painful chapters in God's overall glorious plan

Hallelujah! You just closed a sale!

> **Psalm 84:11 (AMP)**
>
> "For the Lord God is a sun and shield; The Lord bestows grace and favor and honor; No good thing will He withhold from those who walk uprightly."

Reflect: ***Think back over how God first brought you this client. Why do you think God gave you this client and transaction—what was/is The God Layer here? How was God's timing?***

If you've already read the chapter just before this one, you might recognize the same opening words above—our praise and thanks should not change for a difficult transaction. It was still God's plan; He knew the transaction would go the way it did.

Many times in the Bible, God inserts painful chapters into what is a glorious plan overall. Think about the story of Joseph, whose brothers sold him into slavery. God gifted Joseph with the interpretation of dreams and caused him to find favor with the Pharoah of Egypt. Years later, Joseph was the reason his family could stay alive during seven years of famine.

> **Genesis 50:20 (NLT)**
>
> [Joseph to his brothers:] “You intended to harm me, but God intended it all for good. He brought me to this position so I could save the lives of many people.”

It can be easy to miss the forest for the trees during a difficult time, but God’s vast forest is always full of good. Let’s not get so cross-eyed focusing on a few difficult trees that we forget His overall good God Layer. Just because this transaction was tough, doesn’t mean it was all bad—after all, God got you to the finish line!

If the property circumstances were difficult—an upcoming Homeowners’ Association assessment that needed to be negotiated, or snags with the loan approval, for example—learning how to overcome these obstacles gave us new knowledge for our book of experience. Praise God!

If our client relationship made this a difficult transaction, now that the transaction is over, we can ask God for a clear head and calm emotions to know how best to approach our client with love. Our client’s behavior may also change once the transaction is closed—I’ve seen animosity and tension dissipate once the transaction is over. Just as I wrote in the last chapter, an invitation to share a meal can be a friendly way to close this chapter and start a fresh new one with our client.

> **Romans 14:19 (NIV)**
>
> “Let us therefore make every effort to do what leads to peace and to mutual edification.”

If it seems our client doesn’t want any connection with us after the transaction, we may be in a tight spot. But nothing is impossible for God to heal. We can wait for His lead and timing; we can be ready and willing to partner with Him in the future. The God Layer doesn’t stop just because our communication takes a pause. Let's remember that our true purpose in real estate is to love people for the Lord.

1 Corinthians 13:1-8 (NIV)

"If I speak in the tongues of men or of angels, but do not have love, I am only a resounding gong or a clanging cymbal. If I have the gift of prophecy and can fathom all mysteries and all knowledge, and if I have a faith that can move mountains, but do not have love, I am nothing. If I give all I possess to the poor and give over my body to hardship that I may boast, but do not have love, I gain nothing. Love is patient, love is kind. It does not envy, it does not boast, it is not proud. It does not dishonor others, it is not self-seeking, it is not easily angered, it keeps no record of wrongs. Love does not delight in evil but rejoices with the truth. It always protects, always trusts, always hopes, always perseveres. Love never fails."

Reflect: *What is God's next assignment for me with this client?*

Prayer prompt: *Dear Lord, thank you for this transaction. You've taught me many important lessons: __________ and __________. Please show me what your will is next for my relationship with __________. Please shape my heart and attitude to be one with your heart for them; fill me with your unconditional love for them. In your name, Amen.*

Growing your reputation

"Plays well with others"

This last section of the book is about fostering positive relationships with other professionals in our industry: our own team's associates, the loan and escrow officers, attorneys, and cooperating agents—and their teams. We interact with these peers and partners more often than any one client; God calls us to be a light in these relationships also.

> **1 Corinthians 12:18-20 (MSG)**
>
> "As it is, we see that God has carefully placed each part of the body right where he wanted it. But I also want you to think about how this keeps your significance from getting blown up into self-importance. For no matter how significant you are, it is only because of what you are a part of. An enormous eye or a gigantic hand wouldn't be a body, but a monster. What we have is one body with many parts, each its proper size and in its proper place. No part is important on its own."

Reflect: ***Am I guilty of thinking I have more knowledge or importance than others in the transaction? How can I make sure I help all the players in the transaction feel equally important and needed?***

Successful teamwork requires us to have servant-like humility; we must have mutual respect for each player's skill set. It's all too easy for us agents to think we are so important, and all the other players are secondary. No matter how 'big' or 'small' a part each plays, we need the entire team to get us to the closing table.

> **Galatians 6:2-3 (NLT)**
>
> "Share each other's burdens, and in this way obey the law of Christ. If you think you are too important to help someone, you are only fooling yourself. You are not that important."

The very first chapter of this book, "The most important thing," is about integrity and building a good reputation as an agent. It's not about who we know, what brokerage we belong to, or our list of awards and accomplishments. Our reputation is built one phone call, one email, and one transaction at a time. Our industry peers and partners will see our true colors through many seasons.

Reflect: ***When have my actions or words improved my reputation with my industry peers? When were my actions or words detrimental to my reputation?***

Let's find opportunities to compliment and build camaraderie with the other agent. We can initiate a proactive and positive communication environment. If the transaction hits a snag, let's approach conversations with gentleness and a goal of a mutually beneficial solution. It's never helpful to point fingers. Instead, let's rally our industry partners and find solutions together. Let's continuously sharpen our tools, because even the best knife cannot sharpen itself.

> **Proverbs 27:17 (NIV)**
>
> "As iron sharpens iron, so one person sharpens another."

How we act and communicate with our industry associates = our reputation = our effectiveness for Christ.

We have so many chances to spread God's light to our peers in the industry. As we build our reputation as Christ-followers, God will work through us. Just like our kindergarten report card, we want a high score for the "plays well with others" metric. As God grows and blesses our network, let's cherish each relationship for God's glory!

Prayer prompt: *Dear Jesus, as I call myself a Christian and work in real estate, my witness may draw—or repel—those around me. Please help me be mindful each day that I am your representative in my interactions with my peers and partners. Help me keep The God Layer in mind as I become a beacon for you to my peers and partners.*

Showing properties and submitting offers

"Begin with the end in mind"

When we represent a buyer, there are many things we can do before and after showing a property to become the buyer's agent every listing agent wants to work with.

Reflect: ***Have I ever had a great transaction that started off on the right foot, right from the initial showing? How about the opposite, when the communication or showing with the listing agent was a foreboding disaster?***

A pre-showing call gives us intel that can give our buyer an edge. When we make the showing request, we can "begin with the end in mind" (Habit #2 from Steven Covey's bestselling *The 7 Habits of Highly Effective People*). If this ends up being the property our client buys, this listing agent will be in our lives for the next couple of months, so we can strive to make a good impression.

> **Colossians 4:6 (TPT)**
>
> "Let every word you speak be drenched with grace and tempered with truth and clarity. For then you will be prepared to give a respectful answer to anyone who asks about your faith."

If we meet the listing agent at the showing or open house, it's a bonus opportunity to make a solid impression. I encourage my buyers to look around the home while I chat with the agent. It's a good chance to glean information about any disclosures or other offers.

After the showing, we can get in the listing agent's good graces by giving feedback. Even if our buyer isn't interested in pursuing the property, we can show professional courtesy and give timely feedback. When we are on the listing side, don't we appreciate agents who get back to us? Let's build our reputation by becoming known for giving helpful feedback.

> **Galatians 6:9 (NIV)**
>
> "Let us not become weary in doing good, for at the proper time we will reap a harvest if we do not give up."

Prayer prompt: ***Lord, from the first conversation with a listing agent, help me be aware of The God Layer so I can build a positive relationship. Thank you for giving me opportunities to meet and get to know other agents—one conversation and impression at a time.***

If our buyer decides to make an offer, the feedback call can turn into the 'I'm writing an offer' call! Again, keeping the end in mind, let's continue the positive communication. Listing agents are busy, especially if it's a hot market or hot listing; we can be brief but memorable as we gather information to prepare our offer. Depending on the listing agent's style and availability, we may or may not get a prompt—or any—response. But even a busy listing agent will take note of a courteous and respectful buyer's agent; this will help put our offer in a good light.

Client 'love letters' may be illegal or frowned upon in your market, but agent-to-agent communication can still be done in a professional manner by sticking to pertinent facts about your client's qualifications and offer. Your broker can give you the best guidance on best practice when presenting your offer.

When we are writing an offer with a loan, we will also partner with the buyer's loan officer. This is another industry relationship that can outlast the offer or transaction, so let's approach the loan officer with God's love. Tag-teaming with the loan officer also shows a united and cooperative front to the listing agent; our buyer's chances can improve!

As we lay a good foundation with the listing agent or loan officer, we will reap the benefits when our buyer's offer is accepted. We can look for continued opportunities to build rapport for whatever purpose God has planned.

If our offer is not accepted, it's an extra but sometimes forgotten gesture to thank the listing agent for their consideration. We can ask what we could have done better, or inquire about a backup position. We can stay on the listing agent's radar in case something changes with their first buyer.

With showing request apps, the ease of texting, and the phenomenon of real estate teams, we may not pick up the phone and talk with the listing agent as much anymore, let alone meet them in person. Taking the extra step to connect with the listing agent will never be a waste. Nothing we do with The God Layer in mind is ever a waste.

Prayer prompt: *Dear God, help me see and take advantage of all opportunities to connect with listing agents and loan officers. Give me more of your loving spirit as I form relationships in the industry. In Jesus' name, Amen.*

When you have a hot listing

Fair and kind communication

When it's a hot seller's market or you've been blessed with a particularly desirable listing (thank you, Jesus!), the showing requests, questions about the property, and threats of offers from buyers' agents are non-stop. Hallelujah; what a great position to be in!

Reflect: ***What was one of my most popular listings that had a lot of activity and offers? How did I handle the response from buyers and agents? What could I have done differently, or better?***

Being inundated with so many agents' inquiries tests our integrity. We are all susceptible to favoritism, even though we may not intend it. One agent calling is someone we know and like; another is someone about whom we've heard negative rumors, or worked with previously and it wasn't the best experience. One agent tells us their buyer is all cash; another tells us their buyer only has 5% down. None of this matters at this stage; we must be fair and present the same helpful attitude and information to all.

Our job is to attract as many buyers as possible for our sellers' consideration; we never know which agent is going to end up bringing in the winning offer. So, when an agent asks a question that has already been answered in the MLS, or changes their showing time at the last minute, let's smile and be gracious as if this is the agent who is going to bring in the best offer.

Reflect: ***When have I been on the buyer's side for a hot listing? Did the listing***

agent do a good job handling my attempts to communicate with him/her? What can I learn from their good/bad example?

1 Timothy 5:21 (NIV)

"I charge you, in the sight of God and Christ Jesus and the elect angels, to keep these instructions without partiality, and to do nothing out of favoritism."

2 Chronicles 19:7 (MSG)

"Live in the fear of God—be most careful, for God hates dishonesty, partiality, and bribery."

How we conduct ourselves with our peers matters to God. After our seller has made their first choice among the many offers received, we must be faithful in one very important task: making the difficult phone calls to the agents whose offers were not chosen. Let's "clothe [ourselves] with compassion, kindness, humility, gentleness, and patience" (Colossians 3:12) as we break the news. Although we'll have a myriad of other tasks to open escrow, let's respect each buyer's agent's time and effort, and honor them as they wait to hear back from us.

During a crazy seller's market, I had a listing that received over 30 offers. It would have taken me days to call every buyer's agent with the news, so I decided to send one email with all the buyers' agents blind copied. I tried to write with compassion and gratitude: I thanked them for all their hard work, gave the total number of offers, explained the general reasons why the seller chose the winning offer, then encouraged them and their buyers as they continued their search.

It may not have been the ideal way to get back to everyone, but I was relieved to receive many thankful replies. The feedback about the winning offer was something the agents could share with their buyers, and a few mentioned there were times they never heard anything from the listing agent. Even if it's via an email like this, let's be kind and not keep buyers waiting.

> **Matthew 7:12 (NLT)**
>
> "Do to others whatever you would like them to do to you. This is the essence of all that is taught in the law and the prophets."

The listing agents I most respect are those with a consistent generosity of spirit; they are always gracious even if I catch them at a bad time, or if I'm asking the same question five other agents have already asked. It takes self-discipline (biting our tongue) and love. Let's be gracious and grateful when we have a popular listing!

Prayer prompt: *Lord, help me to be respectful and fair to all who inquire about my listing so that I can give the same, fair access to the listing and any helpful information. Thank you for this amazing listing! It is a great opportunity to meet and talk with so many of my agent peers. In your name, Amen.*

The escrow journey

Godly cooperation with our industry partners

Praise God! You and your client are opening escrow! Hopefully you've already started off on the right foot with the other agent during the showing and offer stages. Even if communication hasn't been ideal so far, opening escrow is a chance to start fresh. Let's be the one to set a positive tone and initiate goodwill.

Reflect: ***What are some ways I can initiate or continue good communication with the other agent?***

In the coming transaction, God has called you into a relationship with the other agent and other industry partners. The God Layer will be present and working on all sides. Let's see what God has planned!

> **Amos 3:3 (NLT)**
>
> "Can two people walk together
> without agreeing on the direction?"

Prayer prompt: ***Lord, thank you for the new escrow! I'm excited to see what your God Layer purpose is here. I invite you to be at the center of my relationships and communication with my peers I'll be working with. Help me always be loving in my words and actions.***

We can open the lines of communication with the other agent with a good, old-fashioned phone call. These days, many transactions can happen entirely through email and text, which can render them cooler and more distant. In contrast, when I've been in transaction with an 'old timer' who likes to do everything over the phone, the transaction is warmer and more personable. We can all be 'old souls' for the sake of The God Layer!

Let's let our words be guided by professional respect and warmth. We can start the call with a simple 'thank you' and 'looking forward to working with you.' If we haven't met them yet, we can mention we are looking forward to meeting them at some point during the transaction.

There will most likely be junctures during the transaction where both sides will need to negotiate and reach agreement. If we lay a strong foundation of good communication up front, any bumps along the way will be easier to navigate.

Philippians 4:8-9 (MSG)

"Summing it all up, friends, I'd say you'll do best by filling your minds and meditating on things true, noble, reputable, authentic, compelling, gracious—the best, not the worst; the beautiful, not the ugly; things to praise, not things to curse. Put into practice what you learned from me, what you heard and saw and realized. Do that, and God, who makes everything work together, will work you into his most excellent harmonies."

As our escrow proceeds, let's be responsive to any requests and patient as we wait for replies. Let's not be that frustrating agent who doesn't acknowledge an email, call, or text, or hounds the other side if we don't hear back right away. We are all busy; the agent may not be the one holding up the communication—they might be waiting to hear back from their client.

If a deal-breaking issue arises that can't be overcome, we must not take out any frustration about a cancellation on the other agent. The cancellation talk should be professional and remain full of gratitude. We may cross paths with this agent again in future, so let's be respectful as we do our best to end things on a positive note.

I once had a buyer's agent email a cancellation form with no warning, courtesy call, or explanation. I acknowledged the email, then called her to check in. She was not very forthcoming with me and seemed exasperated and down by the loss of the escrow. Although I had started the call puzzled and a little upset for my seller, God gave me compassion for her. I ended up trying to reassure her she would find her buyer the right home very soon. Let's use our words to encourage and build up our peers.

> **Romans 12:18 (NLT)**
>
> "Do all that you can to live in peace with everyone."

Prayer prompt: ***Dear Jesus, give me more of your love and patience as I work with my peers. Help us develop a rapport that you might use even after this transaction. If there is confrontation, help me calm my temper and hold my tongue; give me the right words—or the control to stay silent. Thank you for always guiding me. In your name, Amen.***

When you're in negotiation

Pure motives

Negotiation with the other side can be a true test, not only of our skills as agents, but our hearts as followers of Christ. We might feel that stretching the truth a little is part of doing our job to serve our client. For example, when we are asked for details about any offers our listing has received, it can be tempting to fudge how many we have, or how strong they might be. But let's not kid ourselves: God hates any kind of dishonesty or embellishment of the truth.

> **Proverbs 16:2 (NLT)**
>
> "People may be pure in their own eyes, but the Lord examines their motives."

Reflect: ***What are some examples of dishonesty or impure motives in negotiation? What could motivate an agent to be dishonest?***

> **2 Corinthians 8:21 (NIV)**
>
> "For we are taking pains to do what is right, not only in the eyes of the Lord but also in the eyes of man."

Prayer prompt: ***God, I need your guidance with this negotiation. You call me to be a bearer of truth. I desire to be honest in all my dealings with other***

agents. Please give me the integrity to choose the right words and actions while representing my client.

Our emotions as agents should not come into play or add to any drama between the seller and buyer. If we are up against an agent who takes a combative stance, one tactic I learned from an excellent agent—my husband, Mike—is to pause and remain silent. Rather than stoking fiery words with a fiery response, silence diffuses any charged emotions (and sometimes freaks the other side out!). Pretty soon, the other side will run out of steam and feel the futility of their outbursts. Once they calm down, we can continue to talk. Don't worry, remaining calm is not the same as agreeing or giving in.

> **Proverbs 15:1 (NLT)**
>
> "A gentle answer deflects anger, but harsh words make tempers flare."

A tough negotiation can strain our relationship with the other agent. An agent who is usually calm and pleasant can become uncharacteristically challenging. Let's remember they may be in a tight spot with a demanding client; everyone feels pressure during a negotiation. If things get heated, let's do our best not to hold the agent's words or actions against them for the sake of our future professional relationship. If we are the ones who acted out of line, let's be quick to apologize.

With a spirit of cooperation, let's be optimistic that we will be able to work things out. If the seller and buyer can't come to terms, we agents should be able to have mutual respect and professional courtesy as we walk away from the failed transaction. Let's pray before and during the tough conversations, and God will help us speak with His kindness and love.

One damaging thing can be if another agent perceives an action we take as dishonest or deceitful, when that wasn't our intention. As we guard our reputation, we should go the extra mile to work out any misunderstandings, even before they might happen.

During the super-competitive 2021 market, to strengthen my buyer's offer against a dozen others, we wrote that the "home inspection is for informational purposes only" (meaning we would not use the inspection results to negotiate any repairs or credits). We wrote this with 100% conviction because we saw from our showing that the home was well-cared for. My buyer's offer was accepted based in part on this concession.

I had worked with the listing agent previously, and when she sent the acceptance, she mentioned she trusted my integrity. I felt motivated to uphold her trust in me. Unfortunately, our home inspection uncovered a major leak that affected a large area of drywall and ceiling. My clients wanted to ask for a credit towards having the leak and affected area repaired after closing. I understood my buyer's position and was 100% ready to support them with their request even though we'd be going against our promise; but I was worried this agent would never trust my word again. My first duty was to my client, but I pleaded with God for some kind of solution that might also preserve trust with the agent.

God answered with an idea (I know it was His idea because I've never done this before during escrow!). I wrote a letter to the agent and her seller to detail the inspection findings. I confessed that the buyers and I were struggling to stay true to our word. With humility, I asked for the credit for repairs on behalf of my client, but also wrote (with my client's permission) that we understood if they held us to our word. Most negotiation experts would advise against adding the second half, but by the grace of God, the seller had mercy and agreed to the credit because they had been unaware of the problem.

The next time we find ourselves stuck, I hope this story will remind us that the Lord will always help us find an honest way; we have a most creative God! Even during the roughest patches in negotiations, we can continue to be professional and pleasant—let's remember we are representatives of the Lord.

Psalm 84:11 (NLT)

"For the Lord God is our sun and our shield. He gives us grace and glory. The Lord will withhold no good thing from those who do what is right."

Prayer prompt: *Dear God, I want my motives to be pure as I negotiate on behalf of my client, __________. I pray the other agent, __________ will see this—and will see you in me. Help me to support my client so they know I am acting for them and their interests. Give me the right stance and truthful words.*

Aggressors and peacemakers

Learning the art of de-escalation

Some transactions can feel like a battle—not with the seller or buyer, but our industry peers. Our emotions and responses can be reactive as we communicate. If the other party is calm and pleasant, it's easy to be nice in return, but if they take an aggressive or combative tone, a natural reaction is to match it; this only escalates things. Over and over in the Bible, God commands us to be at peace with all, and Jesus calls us to prioritize reconciliation.

Matthew 5:22-24 (NLT)

"But I say, if you are even angry with someone, you are subject to judgment! If you call someone an idiot, you are in danger of being brought before the court. And if you curse someone, you are in danger of the fires of hell. So if you are presenting a sacrifice at the altar in the Temple and you suddenly remember that someone has something against you, leave your sacrifice there at the altar. Go and be reconciled to that person. Then come and offer your sacrifice to God."

Ephesians 4:1-3 (NIV)

"... I urge you to live a life worthy of the calling you have received. Be completely humble and gentle; be patient, bearing with one another in love. Make every effort to keep the unity of the Spirit through the bond of peace."

Prayer prompt: *Dear Lord, as I come before you, please calm my emotions. As I read and hear your words today, help me learn to be a peacemaker.*

If an industry peer is aggressive with us over the phone or in person, we can initiate a de-escalation of emotions and language. (Please note that 'calm down' is the worst thing to say; it usually has the opposite effect!) We can choose our words slowly and carefully to create a calmer atmosphere. Hopefully the other person will mirror us, and we can continue with both sides composed and professional.

Written communication can lead to misunderstandings about tone of voice. However, email and text give us time to compose ourselves before replying. Each of us should know our own tendencies—do I tend to regret speaking or texting too quickly? Do I have a better chance of calming down if I take a minute before responding?

If we know from the past that this person can trigger us, we can learn and use a different approach. If I know that this agent's tone of voice can aggravate me and I am the one who becomes combative, I can use email or text communication for any touchy discussions. If I am unsure about the tone of their text or email, I can pick up the phone (after a prayer and a few deep breaths), and make sure there are no misunderstandings.

Reflect: *Who am I sparring with, and how am I feeling about it? Has my communication with this person been effective? What might I try changing to bring us closer to peace?*

Prayer prompt: *Lord, I am having difficulty communicating with __________. I ask for an extra measure of your humility, gentleness, and patience. Please help me initiate a more loving and unifying way of communicating. In your name I pray, Amen.*

> **Matthew 5:9 (NLT)**
>
> "God blesses those who work for peace, for they will be called the children of God."

I had a transaction where I was the aggressor and initiated the combative communication with the loan officer. This loan officer and I were helping a buyer client and had worked together a few times; he is a brother in Christ. Unfortunately, the loan approval process was extremely bumpy and was delaying our closing. In one of my worst moments as an agent, I took my frustration out on my loan officer brother. Although we eventually overcame the issues (which were mostly due to the HOA), I blew the whole situation out of proportion. We ended up closing late after having to ask the seller for several delays, but our client was ecstatic to buy his first condo.

I immaturely cut ties with this loan officer. As I read the passages from Matthew 5 above, I knew God was displeased with me. In His mercy, He gave me an opportunity to reconcile with the loan officer a few years later: our same mutual client had outgrown the one-bedroom condo and wanted to purchase a single-family home with his girlfriend. As we started the new transaction, I asked the loan officer to forgive me for my previous bad behavior, and he graciously did. I am thankful God gave me an opportunity to face my past sin.

The new transaction brought even greater challenges with the loan approval! (I think God wanted me to apply my lesson right away.) This time, God helped me stay focused on the issues at hand instead of who or what had caused them. There wasn't any finger-pointing; the tone of the transaction was completely different—all glory to God! The icing on the cake came on closing day: when I met the buyers at their new home, I became witness to a surprise marriage proposal!

Our clients deserve for us to focus on the positive as much as possible. Let's remember our role as cheerleader and encourager, and not let ourselves or the team become mired in the blame game. We can be arbiters of peace, for the good of The God Layer.

Colossians 3:12-13 (NIV)

"Therefore, as God's chosen people, holy and dearly loved, clothe yourselves with compassion, kindness, humility, gentleness and patience. Bear with each other and forgive one another if any of you has a grievance against someone. Forgive as the Lord forgave you."

Prayer prompt: ***Lord, please make me aware of my shortcomings and the part I play in escalating or de-escalating a situation. Help me be quick to forgive; I want to be the peacmaker you call me to be.***

When you don't know how to solve a problem

The Holy Spirit is our Helper

There are always new situations, players, and problems in real estate—this keeps us on our toes; our job is never boring! It's only natural to stumble into a situation where we don't know what to do.

Reflect: ***What is the problem I'm facing today? Even though God knows everything on your heart and mind, spend some time with the Lord in prayer or by journaling about your predicament. Take time to pause and listen for God's still, small voice of guidance.***

Prayer prompt: ***Lord, I come to you today because I need your wisdom about __________. Help me be still so I can hear your voice.***

Isaiah 11:1-2 (MSG)

"A green Shoot will sprout from Jesse's stump,
  from his roots a budding Branch.
The life-giving Spirit of God will hover over him,
  the Spirit that brings wisdom and understanding,
The Spirit that gives direction and builds strength,
  the Spirit that instills knowledge and Fear-of-God."

The "green Shoot" in this passage is Jesus, and the Holy Spirit is referred to in the passage as the "Spirit of God". The Holy Spirit helped Jesus during His time on earth as a human. We have the same helper: the Holy Spirit is always hovering over us, and lives inside us!

Taken from the Isaiah passage above, the characteristics of the 'Seven-fold Spirit of Jesus' are:

1. The Spirit of the Lord – We are assured the Holy Spirit is of God.
2. The Spirit of Wisdom – The Holy Spirit gives us discernment and the ability to judge what's right and wrong.
3. The Spirit of Understanding – The Holy Spirit gives us comprehension and a grasp of a situation or concept.
4. The Spirit of Counsel – The Holy Spirit guides and gives us a plan.
5. The Spirit of Might – The Holy Spirit gives us the energy, confidence, and power to do something.
6. The Spirit of Knowledge – The Holy Spirit gives us awareness and expertise.
7. The Fear of the Lord – The Fear of the Lord gives us the right perspective: God is God, and we are human.

I can never get enough of this passage, which is why I hope you will return to this chapter whenever you need help. So often we forget we have the helper Holy Spirit as our ultimate resource!

***Reflect**: Which of the 7 characteristics of the Holy Spirit are easy for me to accept? Which have I experienced before? Are any of the 7 difficult for me to grasp? Which of the 7 would really help me today?*

Prayer prompt: *Dear God, thank you for giving me your Holy Spirit to help me. Help me to open my heart and ears to receive your guidance.*

It sounds a little surreal (because it is supernatural!), but there can be times during a transaction when I get an idea, premonition, or burst of insight about the situation. Then I suddenly know exactly what to do, or who to talk to so I can move forward down the path to a solution. This is the Holy Spirit's mysterious, inexplicable work.

Ephesians 1:8 (TPT)

"This superabundant grace is already powerfully working in us, releasing all forms of wisdom and practical understanding."

Prayer prompt: *Dear Holy Spirit, I know along with God the Father and Jesus the Son, you're the third part of the Trinity. I don't always pray directly to you, but today I ask for your seven-fold help (specifically #____, The Spirit of __________) for my situation with __________. Please help me to recognize your supernatural guidance. Help me to know what's right and wrong, and which way to go. Thank you, God!*

When nothing is going right

The source of our strength and stamina

Occasionally, there's a behemoth of a transaction that brings one difficult problem after another. These are the deals that keep us awake at night and we dread waking up to, wondering what new obstacle or development we'll face today.

Reflect: ***What made me turn to this chapter today? What would help reassure me about these challenges?***

Prayer prompt: ***God, help me to see this mess as a somehow blessed mess! I'm feeling __________ and __________. I don't understand why __________. Please give me hope that there will be relief. Please give me faith to entrust these problems to you. In Jesus' name, Amen.***

Our real estate coaches and brokers never promised this job would be a walk in the park. Some new agents look at the job from the outside and think it's glamorous and easy—until they join and discover the many hidden hours of labor and interpersonal challenges.

My first real estate mentor, Abe Lee, said that, unlike a surgeon or an air traffic controller, our problems as agents are not life and death. I would watch Abe navigate challenges and obstacles in transactions, and it always amazed me how he could stay calm through any storm. He'd say, "How is worrying or obsessing over it going to help?" He wasn't being glib or unsympathetic; instead of wasting his breath and sanity with stress, he chooses to reserve his energy and focus for the tasks at hand.

Nothing we face is likely to come close to Paul's years of unjust imprisonment and brushes with death. His intense suffering for the Lord brought him to many a wise conclusion from which we can learn.

> **2 Corinthians 1:8-9 (NIV)**
>
> "We do not want you to be uninformed, brothers and sisters, about the troubles we experienced in the province of Asia. We were under great pressure, far beyond our ability to endure, so that we despaired of life itself. Indeed, we felt we had received the sentence of death. But this happened that we might not rely on ourselves but on God, who raises the dead."

Daily—several times a day—I'm guilty of relying on myself instead of God. But isn't His way better? Let's ask ourselves:

- ~ My limited knowledge, or God's infinite wisdom?
- ~ My faulty, pessimistic ways as a human, or God's ways, which are hopeful and always come from love?
- ~ My limited stamina, or God's unlimited power to sustain me?

When we're facing a mountain of problems, we have a choice: to wallow and wail, or stand up straight and race on. As Paul writes, there will be times of great trouble in life, but God has a reason for leading us to and through them. When we are flailing in our own limited power, God may lead us to hit a wall so we have no other choice but to turn to Him.

2 Samuel 22:29-37 (MSG)

"Suddenly, GOD, your light floods my path,
 GOD drives out the darkness.
I smash the bands of marauders,
 I vault the high fences.
What a God! His road
 stretches straight and smooth.
Every GOD-direction is road-tested.
 Everyone who runs toward him
Makes it.

Is there any god like GOD?
 Are we not at bedrock?
Is not this the God who armed me well,
 then aimed me in the right direction?
Now I run like a deer;
 I'm king of the mountain.
He shows me how to fight;
 I can bend a bronze bow!
You protect me with salvation-armor;
 you touch me and I feel ten feet tall.
You cleared the ground under me
 so my footing was firm."

May this passage energize you when you're facing a volatile situation during a transaction! God gives us challenges so that we turn to Him for help. His plans and ways—His God Layer—are higher. Now let God pull you into His embrace and fill you with His supernatural power to get through!

Prayer prompt: *Dear Jesus, you already know all about my problems. You also know the things I don't know—the things that are yet to come. Thank you for teaching me by making this obstacle so difficult that I must call on you for help. I humbly ask for your wisdom—the perfect real estate wisdom for this situation, Lord! Thank you for carrying me.*

Reflect: *Pause and listen for a word, idea, or picture. As you lay your current problem at His feet, God will show you a way through.*

When you know you were wrong

Don't let the wound fester

I am terribly stubborn; just ask my husband and family. It's monumentally difficult for me to admit when I've been wrong; they are shocked when I actually admit it and ask for forgiveness. I personally need this chapter the most!

Reflect: ***When do I get stubborn? Am I quick or slow to realize I've been wrong?***

I gave some thought to the stages I go through when I've been wrong. Maybe you can relate to this list I came up with:

1. Denial I've done wrong.
2. Questioning whether I've done wrong.
3. Ignoring I've done wrong.
4. Suffering.
5. Knowing I've done wrong, but not yet admitting it.
6. More suffering.
7. Owning up to my mistake.
8. Confessing to God—and receiving His unconditional grace and forgiveness.
9. Confessing to the person I've wronged.
10. Freedom!

I hope you move more quickly to step 7 than I do! If we don't own up to our wrongdoing, we absolutely suffer. The Bible explains this:

Psalm 38:4 (AMP)

"For my iniquities have gone over my head [like the waves of a flood];
As a heavy burden they weigh too much for me."

Psalm 38:4 (MSG)

"I'm swamped by my bad behavior,
collapsed under an avalanche of guilt."

Psalm 32:3-4 (NIV)

"When I kept silent,
my bones wasted away
through my groaning all day long.
For day and night
your hand was heavy on me;
my strength was sapped
as in the heat of summer."

If we love God and want to live in His will, He makes us uncomfortable when we're in the wrong—His hand is heavy on us. If we do not realize and confess our sin, our suffering becomes a wound that festers and infects our whole being—mind, body, and spirit.

Reflect: ***Do I feel the weight of my guilt? Am I ready to make my confession to God and the other person? Am I ready to be restored and healed?***

If you opened this chapter today, you are already at step 7! Now come stages 8 and 9, confessing to God and man; this is where we truly grow as humans and Christians. If we stay stuck suffering with festering wounds, we will not be able to reach God's potential for us as we do His work.

The God Layer is rendered inactive when our pride and sin hold us captive. The faster we can recognize our guilt and share our confessions, the stronger our 'humility muscle' will grow. Let's experience the freedom of confession as soon as possible so we can unlock The God Layer and once again be used by God.

Prayer prompt: ***Dear Lord, I come before you today because I realize I've been stubborn and wrong about __________. I know that because Jesus died for my sins, you forgive me always. Please forgive me and cleanse my heart.***

Let's reread Psalm 32, this time all the way through verse 7:

Psalm 32:3-7 (NIV)

"When I kept silent,
  my bones wasted away
  through my groaning all day long.
For day and night
  your hand was heavy on me;
my strength was sapped
  as in the heat of summer.

Then I acknowledged my sin to you
  and did not cover up my iniquity.
I said, 'I will confess
  my transgressions to the LORD.'
And you forgave
  the guilt of my sin.

Therefore let all the faithful pray to you
  while you may be found;
surely the rising of the mighty waters
  will not reach them.

> You are my hiding place;
> you will protect me from trouble
> and surround me with songs of deliverance."

The art of honest confession is vital to healthy relationships in life and in our work. A successful transaction depends on all involved doing their part and giving each other mutual respect. When there is a breakdown, we have the power to make things right by simply owning up when we were wrong. We know for sure we have God's love and forgiveness. Hopefully our industry partner will also forgive us so we can move forward better and stronger.

Prayer prompt: *God, thank you for breaking down my stubbornness and replacing it with humility. Thank you for giving me the courage to confess to you. Thank you for lifting the burden so I can run your race again and reactivate the work of The God Layer. As I also go to __________ to ask their forgiveness, please give me the right words and opportunity. In Jesus' name, Amen.*

Giving the team credit

Cultivating gratitude

When we finally reach closing day, everyone deserves recognition. It's so easy to give someone a compliment or thanks for a job well done, yet I often forget. Let's not think of ourselves as the most important part of the body; every part is vital. We need the whole team to cross the finish line. This passage of Paul's below is also quoted in Chapter 5-1:

> **1 Corinthians 12:22-23, 25-26 (NLT)**
>
> "In fact, some parts of the body that seem weakest and least important are actually the most necessary. And the parts we regard as less honorable are those we clothe with the greatest care. So we carefully protect those parts that should not be seen... This makes for harmony among the members, so that all the members care for each other. If one part suffers, all the parts suffer with it, and if one part is honored, all the parts are glad."

Reflect: ***What would a transaction look like without the entire team's help? Who is someone I need to recognize today?***

1 Thessalonians 5:11 (MSG)

"So speak encouraging words to one another. Build up hope so you'll all be together in this, no one left out, no one left behind. I know you're already doing this; just keep on doing it."

Prayer prompt: *Dear Lord, thank you for blessing me with great partners on the team like __________ and __________. Please help me find the best way to let them know and feel my appreciation.*

We're usually the most visible member of the team to our client, but let's be sure to introduce and recognize the many hands involved. Everyone deserves to be acknowledged and thanked. We should want—and be proud—to give credit where credit's due.

Thanking the other agent for a mutual success is basic 'professionalism 101.' If there was anything we admired, or something we learned from the other agent's ways, let's happily give them a compliment. On closing day, let's not wait for the other agent to reach out to us; we can be the one to initiate a warm and appreciative call.

It's always good form to be specific when giving praise: 'Thank you for always responding so quickly whenever I asked for anything.' Or, 'I appreciated when you came up with the idea to do XYZ, which made the transaction go so smoothly.' We can spread kindness and respect with genuine words of appreciation.

Romans 14:19 (NIV)

"Let us therefore make every effort to do what leads to peace and to mutual edification."

If there was a breakdown between you and one of the members of the team at some point, now is the time to make amends. Regardless of who did what, or who should ask for forgiveness, let's make the first move toward reconciliation. Even with a cancelled transaction, let's not forget to reach out to our partners even though the transaction failed.

Picking up the phone and taking a few minutes to say thank you can make someone's day. The God Layer hums as we improve our industry relationships. We can build loyalty and friendship—perhaps so much so that God can further their faith. Our ministry absolutely extends to our industry partners.

Prayer prompt: ***Lord, you have blessed me with so many partners and helpers in my work! I thank you for bringing me the right associates to work with, and for the many things I've learned from them. Please help me remember to tell them how much I appreciate them. Please show me which relationships might be ripe for your blessing.***

Giving and receiving referrals

The God Layer in every connection

We refer our buyers to our tried-and-true loan officers and home inspectors; we refer our sellers to the most knowledgeable tradespeople and title officers we know. We enlist these partners to help us serve our clients so we can achieve a successful transaction. These partners may also be an important part of The God Layer.

Reflect: ***When was the last time I referred my client to another professional? How did I choose that person?***

> **1 Corinthians 3:9 (NIV)**
>
> "For we are co-workers in God's service; you are God's field, God's building."

Even as we refer a client to other industry professionals, the Lord is the ultimate assembler of this client's team. I am guilty of running on autopilot and referring every single buyer to the same loan officer (or inspector, etc.). It's not necessarily wrong, but why not spend time in prayer for God's guidance on which loan officer partner He's chosen for this client? The Lord can use believers and non-believers for our clients. Let's not discriminate in this way, and instead remain open to the team God has chosen for each client.

Please also consult with your broker about any company guidelines; they may recommend referring more than one vendor. We should always let the client make the final choice. I had a buyer who needed a real estate attorney to review a tricky encroachment situation. None of my attorney contacts were available in our last-minute time frame, but my clients found someone who came through for us. I can now happily welcome a new partner into my network.

Prayer prompt: ***Dear God, thank you for giving me meaningful relationships with other professionals. Help me to remember you are the ultimate referrer and connector! Please guide me to both give and receive referrals with a prayerful and generous heart. In Jesus' name, Amen.***

Reflect: ***What should my motive be when giving a referral?***

It is self-serving and wrong if we refer clients to industry partners with the motive of receiving referrals from them in return. Let's remember to always consider our clients' best interests—we need to refer them to the partner who will be the right and best fit for them, not the one who might return the favor.

Luke 6:34 (NIV)

"And if you lend to those from whom you expect repayment, what credit is that to you? Even sinners lend to sinners, expecting to be repaid in full."

Let's continue to rely on God for new clients and not pressure our partners for referrals. We can focus on being highly *referrable* by always being professional and courteous—both in transactions and at industry events—and let God award us any referrals in His time and for His purpose. We can network with the purpose of making God Layer connections with our professional peers, and let God open the door when He wants us to work with them.

When an industry colleague honors us with a referral, let's remember to thank them, as well as God! As with each new client, we can spend time in prayer to seek the Lord's purpose in this connection. Then, as we begin to work with the referred client, let's make our colleague proud to have referred us. As He often does, God may have a dual purpose—a mission for us with this new client, as well as a deeper relationship with our industry partner.

2 Corinthians 9:8 (NLT)

"And God will generously provide all you need. Then you will always have everything you need and plenty left over to share with others."

2 Corinthians 9:8 (MSG)

"God can pour on the blessings in astonishing ways so that you're ready for anything and everything, more than just ready to do what needs to be done."

Prayer prompt: *Lord, you are CEO of my business. I trust you will hire the right industry partners, both for my clients' best interests and as friendships/relationships for me to tend. Thank you for knowing the perfect fit for my clients.*

Being a light in the industry

Seeing The God Layer in everything

In early 2022, my husband Mike and I were invited to a Zoom prayer meeting for a broker friend, Jason Nishikawa. Jason had been battling cancer and suffering the side effects of chemotherapy. Despite this, he accepted Jesus and God was using him in incredible ways! Jason saw his illness as an opportunity to witness to friends, family, clients, and peers.

On the Zoom call, I'm sure there were some who weren't of any religion or faith, as well as some Christians whose faith needed a boost. We all certainly received that boost as we witnessed Jason's tremendous peace and trust in the Lord's plan. His powerful testimony left us all praising God. In his words, he felt chosen by God to have cancer so God could use his story. This 'baby' Christian could see so clearly how The God Layer was at work through his life ... can I get an 'Amen'?!

Isaiah 52:7 (MSG)

"How beautiful on the mountains
  are the feet of the messenger bringing good news,
Breaking the news that all's well,
  proclaiming good times, announcing salvation,
  telling Zion, 'Your God reigns!'"

If we are willing, we get to be God's beautiful hands and feet, bringing those around us the Good News. God has chosen each one of us to be His messengers in our broad-reaching real estate industry. His mission for us is to be bearers of His light and salvation to anyone and everyone whose path we cross.

> **Ephesians 1:19 (TPT)**
>
> "I pray that you will continually experience the immeasurable greatness of God's power made available to you through faith. Then your lives will be an advertisement of this immense power as it works through you!"

Reflect: *In which industry or client relationships have I seen The God Layer? How do I see God working through me?*

Prayer prompt: *God, your hand is on everyone and everything; you are all-seeing, all-knowing, and all-powerful. I would like you to use me to enable more people to experience your love and joy. Thank you for placing me in a position of meaningful interaction with so many. Open my eyes and heart to understand your mission for me in each relationship! In Jesus' name, Amen.*

Although this is the last chapter in this book, I hope it's one you'll read often and feel encouraged by God and His goals for us:

- May we see how God is actively working through us in our life and business.
- May God encourage us as we live out our faith at every juncture in real estate.

- May God embolden us to share our faith with our clients and industry peers.
- May we change lives for Jesus and fulfill His great commission to enlarge the body of believers.

1 Corinthians 15:57-58 (MSG)

"It was sin that made death so frightening and law-code guilt that gave sin its leverage, its destructive power. But now in a single victorious stroke of Life, all three—sin, guilt, death—are gone, the gift of our Master, Jesus Christ. Thank God! With all this going for us, my dear, dear friends, stand your ground. And don't hold back. Throw yourselves into the work of the Master, confident that nothing you do for him is a waste of time or effort."

Sadly for us left here on earth, the Lord called Jason to heaven after a valiant, purpose-filled, 19-month battle with cancer. Jason made each day count! He is now in his heavenly body, free from pain and suffering. God welcomed him home with, "Well done, my good and faithful servant."

My husband and I attended the memorial service along with hundreds of others; it was the largest service I've ever had the honor of attending. We heard testimonies from his family and friends, and Proverbs 3:5-6 featured prominently on the front of the program as testimony of his trust in God no matter what. The Holy Spirit was mightily present, making God-impressions on all who were there. When I think about Jason's heart for the Lord and how God was able to reach so many people through him during those months, I can only sing praises of wonder—what an example of giving The God Layer full play!

I pray God opens up God Layer opportunities for all of us to spread His light and love. I would love to hear from you with your testimonies of God's goodness.

Proverbs 3:5-6 (NIV)

"Trust in the Lord with all your heart
and lean not on your own understanding;
in all your ways submit to him,
and he will make your paths straight."

Prayer prompt: *Dear Jesus, thank you for putting me exactly where I am, around the clients and industry partners you've chosen specifically for me. Help me do all I can so others can experience the peace, joy, and relief your salvation brings. Let me always be on the lookout for your God Layer, so I can seize opportunities to be your light! Give me courage and the right words to use with all I meet. In your precious name, Amen.*

Acknowledgements

To my Lord and Savior, Jesus Christ: Thank you giving me the idea and title for the book, and for arranging my schedule—these two years of writing have been a joy and honor. This is Your book—may Your will for it be done!

To my husband, Mike DeMello: Thank you for your unconditional love and patient support.

To Book Designer and brother, Donjiro Ban: Thank you for breathing beauty into this book. Losing mom has been a little easier because we can journey forward together.

To first reader and sister-in-law, Esther Ban: Thank you for making the time to read and give helpful feedback all while nurturing the family.

To Editor, Mary Sayed: I thank God for choosing a soul sister to finesse every word! I hope to meet you someday on this earth, but I know we will meet in heaven—along with our mums.

To Cover Artist, Erika Molyneux: You are a Godsend—thank you for capturing the spirit and message of the book so perfectly for the cover.

To Redfin CEO, Glenn Kelman: Our company's values are kind and good because you are kind and good. Your support of me and this book is everything, thank you.

To first reader, Liz Garcia: Thank you for being a rock of support for this book and its unfolding ministry.

To first reader, Gill Berger: Thank you and Lorelyn for being godly examples for me in business, hospitality, and loving by serving.

To first reader, Cherie Tsukamoto: Thank you for shining God's light to me and all those around you.

To first reader, Rod Mukai: Thank you for always generously giving of your quiet wisdom and leadership.

To first reader, James Chan: Thank you for your encouraging friendship in both faith and real estate.

To first reader, Tim O'Leary: Thank you for being one of my most enthusiastic first readers! I learn so much watching your example of humility.

To first reader, Pastor Amel Dominguez: Thank you for your scholarship and care as you reviewed the Bible references throughout the book.

To first readers, Del and Sean Mochizuki: I respect you both so much and aspire to read as many books as you do! Thank you for previewing this one.

To first reader, Courtney Hara: Thank you for your friendship through ministry in Osaka, your tireless work at HBR, and your transaction that inspired one of my favorite chapters!

To first reader, Shannon Among: Thank you for being the person I call sis. Thanks also for introducing me to your aunt, Dietra M. Cordea—her timely advice was a Godsend.

To the spiritual mentors throughout my life - the late Pastor Bob Westgate, Pastor Kent MacDonald, Karen Lee Seth, Pastor David "Waxer" Tipton, Pastor Makito Matsuda, Pastor Jordan Seng, and Pastor Rick Warren: Thank you for your steadfast service and teaching.

To the business mentors throughout my life - Mike Beveridge, Dean Feldmeier, the late Sandie Arntzen, Bob Taylor, Abe Lee, and John Connelley: Thank you for believing in me.

About the Author ~ A Testimony

My brother, Don, and I were lovingly raised in a Christian home in Lake Oswego, Oregon by our parents, Tatsuya and Yumiko Ban. My mother was a Christian—very rare in Japan—and my father accepted the Lord during a period of isolation recovering from tuberculosis. His faith and fervor for God grew so much that he eventually became a pastor while continuing his home-building and export business.

I spent my 20's and 30's running far away from God. But when I turned 40, that existential question nagged me: what am I doing with my life? Despite outward success as an executive, inside I had nothing substantial. Thankfully, God makes it easy for anyone to become a prodigal son or daughter, and I ran back to His loving arms.

I didn't know what job God was planning for me next, but in early 2011, He prompted me to trust Him and give notice. It was a divine appointment when my last day fell on March 11, 2011, the day of the devastating earthquake and tsunami in northern Japan. God clearly spoke in my heart that morning: my next job was in Japan. I traded my cushy executive lifestyle in paradise for an uncomfortable life in the woods outside Sendai.

During the months I volunteered with a Christian disaster relief organization, God surrounded and taught me through the many who responded in faith from around the world. On Sundays, we were hosted and refreshed by the members of a most vibrant and welcoming church, Oasis Chapel. Then during the week, we served the survivors still living in shelters and grieving their lost loved ones and homes. We heard their regrets and realizations about what is truly important in life—and it wasn't money, status, or things.

One of my last tasks at the volunteer camp was to clean the toilets in the communal log cabin where we lived. I finally understood how to do work that was eternally meaningful: as long as I am showing and sharing God's love with others, He will bring fulfillment to even the most menial work.

So, upon returning to Hawaii, God led me to a career in real estate in which to love and serve others. I became a full-time agent in 2012, a broker in 2015, and moved to Redfin in 2016. I give all credit to God and Redfin's business model for enabling me to complete many transactions in a short time (300 sales in 7 years at Redfin). In hindsight, maybe God's motive was to give me enough experience to prepare me to write this book.

Through my many failures and hard lessons in the business, God showed me His true purpose—His God Layer—for my work. He continues to teach and challenge me as I strive to serve my clients and peers as well as He calls me to. From conception to completion, He is truly behind every word of this book.

Moving to Redfin uncovered another purpose God had for me: meeting (and marrying, in 2017) my husband, Mike DeMello. He, too, is behind every word of this book: he freely shares his real estate knowledge with me; he is patient and gracious to allow me the countless hours to write; and he loves me unconditionally while witnessing my constant failure to practice the godly words and actions I write about.

What is God planning for me next? Two things I know: I will continue to serve my real estate clients, and my next book is dedicated to them: *Faith Lessons for Home Sellers and Buyers.*

To all my brothers and sisters in real estate. Thank you for caring for your clients and peers and seeking God's best for them. From the bottom of my heart, thank you for reading!

Ali

December 2023

A Note from the Cover Artist

I teach printmaking and new media arts at Leeward Community College and paint regularly on the art ministry team at my church, Bluewater Mission, on the island of Oahu, Hawai'i.

Art ministry has been an ongoing journey of stepping out in faith and vulnerability to connect with God in real time and use the gifts I have been given. As a creative on this prophetic team, I actively listen for the voice of God, then create images according to visions and words I receive to bless others with affirmation, direction, inspiration, hope, faith, and tangible visual mementos. The entire process takes place during church services. To step into this role, I had to reframe both how and why I was creating work to fit the context. The time frame is short, and the act of publicly creating artwork initially gave me anxiety. To grow, I needed to let go of perfectionist qualities and focus completely on the act as an offering of worship and faith.

Author Ali Ban originally contacted me after being moved by some of my prophetic art ministry paintings. For the cover of The God Layer, my hope is to offer an eye-catching image that will evoke the sense of grace, privilege, and freedom that come with practicing faith in one's professional life. I am excited for God to bless you with this exciting, faith-filled, practical guidebook.

Erika Molyneux

Contact the Author:

Ali welcomes your questions, comments, and praise reports!

Email:

Ali@ForTheGoodPublishing.com

Phone:

808-227-8030

Please check Ali's website to find bonus chapters, discussion questions, and other resources for mentor and peer groups.

Website:

ForTheGoodPublishing.com

Index

Topic *Section–Chapter*